Crystallization-Study
of the
Minor
Prophets

Volume Two

Witness Lee

The Holy Word for Morning Revival

Living Stream Ministry
Anaheim, CA • www.lsm.org

First Edition, August 2012.

ISBN 978-0-7363-6228-3

Published by

Living Stream Ministry
2431 W. La Palma Ave., Anaheim, CA 92801 U.S.A.
P. O. Box 2121, Anaheim, CA 92814 U.S.A.

Printed in the United States of America

12 13 14 15 / 5 4 3 2 1

2012 Summer Training

CRYSTALLIZATION-STUDY OF THE MINOR PROPHETS

Contents

Preface

1. This book is intended as an aid to believers in developing a daily time of morning revival with the Lord in His word. At the same time, it provides a limited review of the summer training held July 2-7, 2012, in Anaheim, California, on the "Crystallization-study of the Minor Prophets." Through intimate contact with the Lord in His word, the believers can be constituted with life and truth and thereby equipped to prophesy in the meetings of the church unto the building up of the Body of Christ.

2. The entire content of this book is taken from *Crystallization-study Outlines: The Minor Prophets,* the text and footnotes of the Recovery Version of the Bible, selections from the writings of Witness Lee and Watchman Nee, and *Hymns,* all of which are published by Living Stream Ministry.

3. The book is divided into weeks. One training message is covered per week. Each week presents first the message outline, followed by six daily portions, a hymn, and then some space for writing. The training outline has been divided into days, corresponding to the six daily portions. Each daily portion covers certain points and begins with a section entitled "Morning Nourishment." This section contains selected verses and a short reading that can provide rich spiritual nourishment through intimate fellowship with the Lord. The "Morning Nourishment" is followed by a section entitled "Today's Reading," a longer portion of ministry related to the day's main points. Each day's portion concludes with a short list of references for further reading and some space for the saints to make notes concerning their spiritual inspiration, enlightenment, and enjoyment to serve as a reminder of what they have received of the Lord that day.

4. The space provided at the end of each week is for composing a short prophecy. This prophecy can be composed by considering all of our daily notes, the "harvest" of our inspirations during the week, and preparing a main point with

some sub-points to be spoken in the church meetings for the organic building up of the Body of Christ.

5. Following the last week in this volume, we have provided reading schedules for both the Old and New Testaments in the Recovery Version with footnotes. These schedules are arranged so that one can read through both the Old and New Testaments of the Recovery Version with footnotes in two years.

6. As a practical aid to the saints' feeding on the Word throughout the day, we have provided verse cards at the end of the volume, which correspond to each day's Scripture reading. These may be cut out and carried along as a source of spiritual enlightenment and nourishment in the saints' daily lives.

7. *Crystallization-study Outlines: The Minor Prophets* was compiled by Living Stream Ministry from the writings of Witness Lee and Watchman Nee. The outlines, footnotes, and cross-references in the Recovery Version of the Bible are by Witness Lee. All of the other references cited in this publication are from the published ministry of Witness Lee and Watchman Nee.

Summer Training
(July 2-7, 2012)

CRYSTALLIZATION-STUDY
OF THE MINOR PROPHETS

Banners:

God's economy in His loving chastisement of Israel,
in His governmental dealing with Israel,
and in His judgment upon the nations
issues in the manifestation of Christ as the centrality
and universality in God's economy
to bring in the kingdom, the age of restoration.

We believers in Christ are members of the Body
of Christ as the organism of the Triune God,
and we should aspire to be the overcomers, -
the mighty ones, who will enlarge
the manifestation of Christ by walking according
to the mingled spirit, who will return with Christ
to deal with Antichrist at the battle of Armageddon,
and who will be His co-kings in the millennium.

The church as the house of Jehovah,
the Father's house, is the dwelling place of God—
the place where God can have His satisfaction
and rest and where God lives and moves to accomplish His will, to satisfy the desire of His heart,
and to carry out His eternal economy
to consummate the New Jerusalem
as His eternal goal for His eternal expression.

We can live in the divine history
within human history
and enter into a new revival to end this age
by arriving at the highest peak
of the divine revelation
of the eternal economy of God through the ministry
of the age, by living the life of a God-man,
and by shepherding people according to God
for the building up of the church as the house of God,
the mutual abode of God and man.

Christ Coming Back as the Real David
to Restore His Kingdom

Scripture Reading: Amos 9:11-12; Hosea 3:5; Micah 4:1-5;
Rev. 3:7

Day 1　　**I. The prophets spoke of David and Christ as one (Jer. 30:9; Ezek. 34:23-24; 37:24-25; Hosea 3:5; Amos 9:11):**

A. God's response to David in 2 Samuel 7:12 made Christ one with David and with David's seed.

B. David's house refers to Christ, David's kingdom refers to Christ's kingdom, and David's throne refers to Christ's throne; the kingdom of David is Christ's kingdom, and David and Christ have one throne (Isa. 9:7; 16:5; Luke 1:32; Acts 2:29-31).

C. "They will serve Jehovah their God and David their King, whom I will raise up for them" (Jer. 30:9); this refers to Christ, who is the real David and who will be the King in the restoration, that is, the millennium (Isa. 32:1; Rev. 20:4, 6).

D. "I will set up over them one Shepherd, My Servant David, and He will feed them; He will feed them, and He will be their Shepherd...And My Servant David will be a Prince among them" (Ezek. 34:23-24):

1. The one Shepherd is Christ, who, as the real David, is the real Shepherd of God's flock and the King of God's people (John 10:11; Heb. 13:20; Isa. 9:7; Hosea 3:5; Micah 5:2; Luke 1:32-33).

2. When the Lord Jesus comes as the Shepherd to care for us, He comes also as the King to govern us; the issue of the Lord's caring for us as our Shepherd is that we obey Him as our King and come under His kingship and throne within us (Ezek. 34:23-24; 37:24).

3. In relation to Israel, the prophecy given in

Ezekiel 34:23-24 will be fulfilled in the age of restoration (Micah 4:1-5).

E. "Afterward the children of Israel will return and seek Jehovah their God and David their King, and they will come with fear to Jehovah and to His goodness in the last days" (Hosea 3:5):

1. "David their King" is Christ in the millennium.

2. *The last days* refers to the age of restoration (Matt. 19:28).

Day 2   **II. Christ is not only the Root of David (Rev. 5:5), the seed of David (Rom. 1:3), and the son of David (Matt. 1:1)—Christ is also the real David (12:3-4):**

A. In keeping with the principle seen in Matthew 12, that Christ is greater than all the types, greater than all things and persons in the Old Testament that typify Him, Christ is the greater David (vv. 6, 38-42).

B. The Lord's word in Matthew 12:3-4 implies that He is the real David; David and his followers are a type of Christ and His disciples.

C. In Matthew 1:6 David is called "the king" because through him, as the conclusion of one age and the beginning of another age, the kingship was brought in; as the real David, the greater David, Christ is such a landmark.

Day 3   **III. "In that day I will raise up / The fallen tabernacle of David, / And I will wall up its breaches / And raise up its ruins / And build it up as it was in the days of old" (Amos 9:11):**

A. The tabernacle of David is the kingdom and the royal family of David (v. 11; Acts 15:16-18):

1. In ancient times the royal family and the kingdom were one; David's kingdom was David's royal family.

2. When Nebuchadnezzar burned Jerusalem and destroyed the temple, that was the fall of the kingdom of David and the royal family of David (2 Kings 25:1-21).

    3. In Amos 9:11 God came in to promise that one day He would raise up "the fallen tabernacle of David," that is, restore the fallen kingdom of David; in that day the kingdom of David and the family of David will be restored, and all the nations will be called by the name of Jehovah (v. 12).

B. Amos 9:11-12 indicates that Christ will come back to be the real David and will rebuild, restore, the kingdom of His forefather David for the restoration of the entire universe; at that time the kingdom of David will become the kingdom of Christ and of God for eternity (Isa. 9:7; 16:5; Jer. 30:9; Mark 11:10; Rev. 11:15):

    1. This prophecy will be fulfilled in the millennial kingdom, in which all the nations will be called by the name of Jehovah and will belong to God and be God's people (Amos 9:11-12; Matt. 13:41; Mark 11:10).

Day 4
&
Day 5

    2. The millennial kingdom will have a heavenly part and an earthly part (Matt. 13:41, 43; Mark 11:10; Luke 1:32-33; Acts 1:6; 2 Sam. 7:12-13):

      a. The heavenly part of the millennial kingdom will be the kingdom of the Father, where the overcomers will reign with Christ as co-kings (Matt. 13:43; Rev. 2:26-27; 3:21-22; 20:4, 6).

      b. The earthly part of the millennial kingdom will be the kingdom of the Son of Man, the kingdom of the Messiah, the tabernacle of David (Matt. 13:41; Rev. 11:15; 2 Sam. 7:13; Amos 9:11):

        (1) This will be the restored nation of Israel, the kingdom of David, for the saved Jews (Acts 1:6; Mark 11:10; Luke 1:32-33; 2 Sam. 7:12-13).

        (2) In the restored kingdom of David, Christ as the Son of Man, David's royal descendant, will be the King over the children of Israel (Amos 9:11; Matt. 1:1; 19:28; 25:31).

IV. **As those who are living in the church as the kingdom of God today, we need to know and experience Christ, the real David, as the One who has the key of David (Rev. 1:4-6; 3:7; Isa. 22:22):**

A. David fought for God, established the kingdom, and prepared everything for the building of the holy temple; as the one who represented God in establishing His kingdom on earth, David had a key—the key of God's dominion (1 Chron. 28:1-8; 29:1-9).

B. The key of David is the key of the kingdom, God's key for ruling the universe (Isa. 22:22; Rev. 3:7).

Day 6   C. The real David is Christ, the One who built the church and established God's kingdom, in which He exercises full authority to represent God (Matt. 16:18-19; 28:18; Gen. 1:26):

1. In His ascension the resurrected Christ is seated at the right hand of the Majesty on high as the Leader of the universe, having the authority to rule sovereignly over all things (Acts 2:34-36; 5:31; 10:36; Heb. 1:3, 13).

2. Christ holds the key of David, that which represents God and opens the whole universe for God (Rev. 3:7).

3. As the One who has the key of David, Christ has the authority to open and shut so that He may establish God's kingdom, God's dominion, and build up God's dwelling place, God's temple (Matt. 16:18-19).

4. The ascended Christ has the key of David in order to give the church in Philadelphia, a type of the recovered church, an opened door so that people can enter the recovered church to be transformed into pillars in the temple of God and to be built up as God's city, the New Jerusalem (Rev. 3:7-8, 12).

Morning Nourishment

Jer.   But they will serve Jehovah their God and David
30:9   their King, whom I will raise up for them.
Hosea Afterward the children of Israel will return and seek
3:5   Jehovah their God and David their King, and they
       will come with fear to Jehovah and to His goodness
       in the last days.

In 2 Samuel 7:12 God was actually telling David that instead of building something for God, he needed God to build His Son into him. It is a marvelous fact that eventually David's seed would be called the Son of God (Rom. 1:3). This indicates the principle of incarnation. Christ is the God-man. As God, He is the Son of God; as man, He is our seed. If the Son of God is not constituted into us, we are nothing. The Son of God must become our seed, yet He remains the Son of God.

In order to work Himself into us, God first became a man through incarnation. As a man He died for us, and then rose up from among the dead and became the life-giving Spirit (1 Cor. 15:45b). This life-giving Spirit is our Savior, who redeemed us on the cross and who is now saving us in our spirit. He is our Redeemer, Savior, life, and seed. As such a One, He is now being built, constituted, into us, making us a part of Him, even as He has made Himself a part of us. (*Life-study of 1 & 2 Samuel,* pp. 154-155)

Today's Reading

If we read 2 Samuel 7 under God's enlightening, we will see that the seed of David is Christ. According to verse 7 God will establish David's kingdom, which refers to Christ's kingdom. This means that the kingdom of David is Christ's kingdom. The prophets spoke of David and Christ as one. In Hosea 3:5 and Amos 9:11 the coming of King David refers to Christ's coming.

In 2 Samuel 7:16 God said to David, "Your house and your kingdom will be made sure forever before you; your throne will be established forever." Here "your kingdom" refers to Christ's kingdom, and "your throne" refers to Christ's throne. In the Bible David and Christ have one throne. Christ is the real David

(Matt. 12:3-6). Eventually, Christ and we become one, for in a very real sense Christ has become us. He is the Head and we are the Body, and the Head and the Body are one. (*Life-study of 1 & 2 Samuel*, pp. 155-156)

[In Jeremiah 30:9 *David their King* refers] to Christ, who is the real David (see note 16[1] in 2 Sam. 7) and who will be the King in the restoration, that is, the millennium (Isa. 32:1; Rev. 20:4, 6). David was a type of Christ as the King. (Jer. 30:9, footnote 1)

When the Lord Jesus comes as the Shepherd to care for us, He comes also as the King to govern us. The issue of the Lord's caring for us as our Shepherd is that we obey Him as our King and come under His kingship and His throne within us. (Ezek. 34:24, footnote 1)

Later, as Hosea 3:5 reveals, the children of Israel will return and seek Jehovah and David their king (Christ in the millennium—Rev. 20:4, 6), and they will come with fear to Jehovah and to His goodness in the latter days (in the restoration age—Matt. 19:28). What Hosea did in obedience to God's command regarding Gomer was a confirmation of what God promised to do regarding Israel. God told Hosea to love Gomer again as a symbol of His intention to love Israel again. Today Israel is a Gomer, but the day is coming when God will restore her to Himself. This restoration will be the result of the manifestation of Christ. Once again I would emphasize the fact that in the prophetic books four things are covered repeatedly: God's chastisement on the Jews, God's punishment upon the nations, the manifestation of Christ, and the restoration. God's chastisement and punishment will issue in the manifestation of Christ, and the manifestation of Christ will bring in the age of restoration, the millennial kingdom, which ushers the old and ruined universe into the new heaven and new earth with the New Jerusalem. If we see these four things, we will see what a hope we have in Christ. (*Life-study of Hosea*, p. 23)

Further Reading: Life-study of 1 & 2 Samuel, msg. 23; *Life-study of Hosea*, msgs. 3-4

Enlightenment and inspiration: _____

_____

_____

_____

Morning Nourishment

Matt. **But He said to them, Have you not read what**
12:3-4 **David did when he became hungry, and those who**
       were with him; how he entered into the house of
       God, and they ate the bread of the Presence, which
       was not lawful for him to eat, nor for those who
       were with him, except for the priests only?
1:6 **And Jesse begot David the king....**

Christ is not only the Root of David (Rev. 5:5), the seed of David (Rom. 1:3), and the Son of David (Matt. 1:1); He is also the real David. In keeping with the principle seen in Matthew 12, that Christ is greater than all the types, greater than all things and persons in the Old Testament that typify Him, Christ is the greater David. (*The Conclusion of the New Testament,* p. 469)

Today's Reading

When the Pharisees criticized the Lord's disciples for picking ears of grain on the Sabbath, He said, "Have you not read what David did when he became hungry, and those who were with him; how he entered into the house of God, and they ate the bread of the Presence, which was not lawful for him to eat, nor for those who were with him, except for the priests only?" (Matt. 12:3-4). The Lord's word implies that He is the real David. In ancient times David and his followers, when rejected, entered into the house of God and ate the bread of the Presence, seemingly breaking the Levitical law. The real David and His followers were also rejected and took action to eat, seemingly against the sabbatical regulation. This indicates that King David was a type of Christ, the real David. David had followers, and Christ, the real David, also had disciples as His followers. King David, God's anointed (1 Sam. 16:13), and his followers were rejected by the people, and the real David, God's Anointed (Heb. 1:9), and His followers were rejected also. Just as David and his followers were hungry, so Christ and His disciples also were hungry. Furthermore, neither David and his followers nor Christ and His followers had anything to eat, but there was the place where there was something to eat. For David it was the house of God, and for Christ it was the grainfields. All this implies that David and his followers were a type, a prefigure, of Christ and His disciples.

The Lord's word in Matthew 12:3 and 4 also implies the dispensational change from the priesthood to the kingship. The coming of David changed the dispensation from the age of the priests to the age of the kings, in which the kings were above the priests. By the coming of Christ the dispensation was also changed, this time from the age of the law to the age of grace, in which Christ is above all. In Matthew 1:6 David is called "the king" because through him the kingdom with the kingship was brought in. He was the landmark of two ages, the conclusion of one age and the beginning of another age. As the real David, the greater David, Christ is such a One. As typified by David, Christ is the fighting King, who has won the victory over all enemies, who has gained the land, and who has prepared all the materials for building up the church as the temple of God. (*The Conclusion of the New Testament,* pp. 469-470)

In the age of the priests, the leader of the people should listen to the priest (Num. 27:21-22). But in the age of the kings, the priest should submit to the king (1 Sam. 2:35-36). Hence, what King David did with his followers was not illegal....Whatever [Christ] did was right. The matter of keeping the Sabbath belonged to the old dispensation of the law. But in the age of grace Christ has the final word. It is not a matter of the law, but of Christ. Therefore, the Lord seemed to be saying to the Pharisees, "You shouldn't condemn Me or My disciples. It is no longer the law that gives the final word, but I, the Christ, I give you the final word. I am the real King, the real David. I am also the Christ who has brought in the dispensation of grace. Thus, whatever I say or do is the final decision." Supposedly the Pharisees knew the Bible, but here they clearly lost the case. How strong was the Lord's defense! (*Life-study of Matthew,* p. 397)

Further Reading: The Conclusion of the New Testament, msg. 44; *Life-study of Matthew,* msg. 32*

Enlightenment and inspiration: _____

_____

_____

Morning Nourishment

Amos **In that day I will raise up the fallen tabernacle of**
9:11-12 **David, and I will wall up its breaches and raise up**
its ruins and build it up as *it was* in the days of old;
that they may possess the remnant of Edom and all
the nations which are called by My name, declares
Jehovah who does this.

This portion of Amos [9:11-12] is quoted by James in Acts 15,
when the apostles and the elders were gathered together to solve
the problem of circumcision.

The tabernacle of David is the kingdom and the royal family
of David. In ancient times it was hard to separate the royal family from the kingdom. Actually these two things are one. David's
kingdom was David's royal family. That kingdom, that royal
family, fell when Nebuchadnezzar came to capture the nation of
Israel, devastate the land, burn the city, destroy the temple, and
carry off the king. That was the fall of the kingdom of David
and the royal family of David. However, in Amos God came in to
promise that some day He would come back to restore the fallen
kingdom of David. In that day the kingdom of David and the
family of David will be restored, and all the nations will be called
by the name of Jehovah. (*Life-study of Amos,* p. 18)

Today's Reading

This prophecy in Amos [9:11-12] indicates that one day Christ
will come back to be the real David. When Christ comes back, in
His last appearing He will be the real David to restore His kingdom and His royal family. That will be the millennial kingdom, in
which all the nations will be called by the name of Jehovah, that
is, all the nations will belong to God. It was based on this that in
Acts 15 James told the Jewish believers not to be bothered by
Peter's and Paul's going to the Gentiles, because in the restoration
all the Gentiles will belong to God, just like the Jews.

Christ will come and restore the fallen kingdom of David to
set up His kingdom for the restoration of the entire universe. At
that time all the nations will become God's people. This is a great

item in Amos's prophecy. (*Life-study of Amos,* p. 18)

The kingdom of God was only drawing near during the time when John the Baptist and the Lord Jesus were preaching (Matt. 3:2; 4:17; Luke 10:9). Although the descending of the Holy Spirit brought in the reality of the kingdom of God on the day of Pentecost and the church was established (Matt. 16:18-19), the manifestation of the kingdom of God was yet to come. Therefore, the Lord was resurrected from the dead and ascended to the heavens to receive the kingdom (Luke 19:12). At the end of the church age, the Lord will receive the kingdom from God (Dan. 7:13-14) and will come back with the kingdom of God (Luke 19:15). That will occur after the great tribulation when the kingdom of the world will become the kingdom of our Lord and of His Christ (Rev. 11:15; 12:10). This will also be the manifestation of the kingdom of God, as unveiled by the Lord on the Mount of Olives in Matthew 24 and 25. This manifested kingdom of God is the millennial kingdom in the coming age, comprising the heavenly and earthly parts....The heavenly part of the millennial kingdom in the coming age, which will be the manifestation of the kingdom of the heavens within the kingdom of God, is called the kingdom of the Father in Matthew 13:43. All the perfected and overcoming saints of the Old and the New Testaments will be priests of God and of Christ, and will be co-kings with Christ for a thousand years (Rev. 20:4, 6) to reign over the nations, the people in the earthly part of the millennial kingdom (Rev. 2:26-27). Daniel 12:2-3 tells us that after being raised up from among the dead, the wise shall shine as the brightness of the firmament, and they that turn many to righteousness shall shine as the stars. This word resembles that in Matthew 13:43, which says that the righteous shall shine forth as the sun in the kingdom of their Father. What is mentioned in Daniel refers also to the heavenly part of the millennial kingdom. (*Truth Lessons—Level One,* vol. 2, pp. 164-165)

Further Reading: Life-study of Amos, msg. 3; *Truth Lessons— Level One,* vol. 2, lsn. 23; *Life-study of Jeremiah,* msg. 20

Enlightenment and inspiration: _____

_____

_____

_____

Morning Nourishment

Matt. Then the righteous will shine forth like the sun in
13:43 the kingdom of their Father....
25:31 But when the Son of Man comes in His glory and
all the angels with Him, at that time He will sit on
the throne of His glory.

In the millennial kingdom there will be three peoples. The first
are the overcoming saints, including the overcoming saints of both
the Old Testament and the New Testament. These overcoming
saints will be co-kings of Christ. Christ is the highest King, and we
shall be His sub-kings. Therefore, the upper section is the royal
portion of the millennium. (*Life-study of Revelation*, p. 648)

Today's Reading

The second group, found in the lower section, is the preserved
and proper Jews, who will be saved at the time of the Lord's coming
back. According to Zechariah 12:10-14, these Jews will look on Him
whom they have pierced, and then they will repent. These are the
Jews who will be the third part who will pass through fire and be
refined (Zech. 13:9). These saved Jews will enter into the millennium as priests and will teach the nations to seek God and to know
Him. Isaiah 2:2-3 will be fulfilled at that time. Verse 3 says, " And
many peoples will come and say, / Come and let us go up to the
mountain of Jehovah, / To the house of the God of Jacob, / That He
may instruct us in His ways, / And that we may walk in His paths. /
For from Zion will go forth instruction, / And the word of Jehovah
from Jerusalem." The nations will learn of God through the instruction of the Jews, who will be priests. Isaiah 61:6 clearly says,
"But you will be called the priests of Jehovah; / People will speak of
you as the ministers of our God." This word will also be fulfilled
during the millennium, when the nations will recognize the Jews
as God's priests.

Zechariah 8:23 says, "...In those days, from all the languages
of the nations, ten men will take hold, indeed, they will take hold
of the skirt of a Jewish man, saying, Let us go with you, for we
have heard that God is with you." This verse indicates that every

Jew will be precious. At that time the number of the saved Jews will be so small that ten people out of one nation will take hold of a Jew and say, "Help us to know God. We want to be taught by you because we have heard that God has blessed you. We want to share your blessing. Tell us about God and teach us how to worship Him." In those days the Jews will be warmly welcomed.

The third group of people in the millennial kingdom will be the "sheep" of Matthew 25. We have seen that these "sheep" will be transferred into the millennial kingdom to become the citizens there. In the lower section of the millennium, called the kingdom of the Son of Man, Jesus as the seed of David will be King over the Jews and, through the Jews, over all the nations. He will be on the throne of David to be the King over all nations through the Jews. This is the kingdom of the Son of Man and the kingdom of the Messiah; it is also the tabernacle of David spoken of in Acts 15:16. The tabernacle of David has fallen. But when the millennium comes, Christ will again erect the tabernacle of David. The tabernacle of David is the kingdom of David. In 2 Samuel 7 God promised to establish David's kingdom forever (v. 16). This everlasting kingdom will be the lower part of the millennium, the kingdom of the Son of Man and of the Messiah. The kingly overcomers will be in the upper part of the millennium, and the priestly Jews and the citizens will be in the lower part.

It is a great help to be clear about these matters. If you understand them, then as you read the Bible, you will know which verses refer to the upper part and which verses to the lower part. You will know which verses refer to the kings, which to the priests, and which to the nations. (*Life-study of Revelation*, pp. 648-650)

In the earthly part is the restored kingdom of David, where Christ as the Son of Man, David's royal descendant, will be the King over the children of Israel. (*The Basic Revelation in the Holy Scriptures*, p. 96)

Further Reading: Life-study of Revelation, msg. 56; *The Conclusion of the New Testament*, msg. 427

Enlightenment and inspiration: _____

_____

_____

_____

Morning Nourishment

Isa. And I will set the key of the house of David upon
22:22 his shoulder—when he opens, no one will shut;
when he shuts, no one will open.
Rev. ...These things says the Holy One, the true One, the
3:7 One who has the key of David, the One who opens and
no one will shut, and shuts and no one opens.
1:6 And made us a kingdom, priests to His God and Father...

The kingdom of a thousand years is different from the New Testament church. There are no Old Testament saints in the church age, but in the kingdom of a thousand years, the overcoming Old Testament saints are present with the overcoming New Testament saints. The kingdom of a thousand years includes Old Testament saints such as Abraham, Noah, Moses, David, and Elijah. These were some of the ones who were overcoming in the Old Testament times. (*The Apostles' Teaching,* p. 127)

Today's Reading

Just before the Lord was transfigured on the mount, He told His disciples, "There are some of those standing here who shall by no means taste death until they see the Son of Man coming in His kingdom" (Matt. 16:28). This was fulfilled by the Lord's transfiguration on the mountain (17:1-3), which was His "coming in His kingdom." It was seen by His three disciples, Peter, James, and John. Furthermore, Moses and Elijah were there conversing with the Lord. His transfiguration there prefigured the coming kingdom. Moses and Elijah represent the Old Testament overcomers who will be in the manifestation of the kingdom, whereas Peter, James, and John represent the New Testament overcomers. The ones selected to reign as kings in the kingdom of a thousand years will be the overcomers, the perfected ones....In the church age, God works Himself into man....The coming kingdom age will be the result of God's work in the church age. (*The Apostles' Teaching,* pp. 127-128)

The all-inclusive Christ, as typified by Eliakim [in Isaiah 22], is also the One upon whose shoulder the key of (the treasury of) the house of God (typified by the house of David for the building up of the kingdom of God) is set (Isa. 22:22; Rev. 3:7). The house of David was for the establishment of the kingdom of David, and the house of God is for the establishment of the kingdom of God. Second Samuel 7:16 indicates that David's house was for his kingdom. Today God's house is for God's kingdom. The church is God's house (1 Tim. 3:15), and the church is also the kingdom of God (Matt. 16:18-19; Rom. 14:17). The kingdom of God is not that evident today because the house of God has not been strongly and adequately built up. When the church as the house of God is adequately built up, the church is manifested as the kingdom of God.

Christ today holds the key of this house, this kingdom. Isaiah 22:22 says that Jehovah would set the key of the house of David upon Eliakim's shoulder. It does not say that Eliakim holds the key but that the key is set upon his shoulder. This expression indicates that this key is a great key. A small key is merely held by someone; it is not put upon his shoulder. The key that God has put on the shoulder of Christ is a great one. Such a big key indicates that the door which it opens is big and thick. Such a door would be a stronghold to protect and keep the treasures of the house of God.

The key is for the keeping of the treasures of the house of God. The treasures today in the house of God are all the riches of Christ. (*Life-study of Isaiah,* pp. 292-293)

The fulfillment of this prophecy [in Isaiah 22:22] is confirmed in Revelation 3:7, because the Lord calls Himself "the Holy One, the true One, the One who has the key of David, the One who opens and no one will shut, and shuts and no one opens." David fought for God, established the kingdom, and prepared everything for the building of the holy temple. Christ the King-Savior is the real David (Matt. 12:3). (*Truth Lessons— Level Four,* vol. 1, p. 110)

Further Reading: The Apostles' Teaching, ch. 11; *Life-study of Isaiah,*
  msg. 42; *Crucial Truths in the Holy Scriptures,* vol. 6, ch. 60

Enlightenment and inspiration: _____
_____
_____
_____

Morning Nourishment

Matt. And Jesus came and spoke to them, saying, All author-
28:18 ity has been given to Me in heaven and on earth.

Rev. **He who overcomes, him I will make a pillar in the**
3:12 **temple of My God, and he shall by no means go out**
anymore, and I will write upon him the name of My
God and the name of the city of My God, the New
Jerusalem, which descends out of heaven from My
God, and My new name.

According to Genesis 1, when God created man, He gave him
dominion over all creatures. This indicates that in God's intention
man is to be the power representing God on earth. Due to the fall,
however, man lost this power and has never fully recovered it.
The key held by David is the key of God's dominion. (*The Conclusion of the New Testament*, p. 413)

Today's Reading

God's dominion includes the entire universe, especially mankind. This dominion has a key that is possessed by the person
[David] who fought the battle for the kingdom and who made prep-
arations for the building of the temple....David represented God in
establishing God's kingdom on earth. Hence, he had the key of
God's dominion in the universe. David, however, was just a type,
not the reality. The real David is Christ, the greater David. He is
the One who built God's temple, the church, and established God's
kingdom. Therefore, in the church today, which is both a house and
a kingdom, we have God's expression and representation. As the
greater David, Christ has built up the house of God, the real temple, and He has set up the kingdom of God, the dominion in which
He exercises full authority to represent God. Therefore, he holds
the key of David..., [which] is something representing God to open
the whole universe for God. This is the key of David held by Christ.
The fact that Christ has the key of David signifies that Christ is the
center of God's economy. He is the One who expresses God and represents Him, the One who holds the key to open everything in

God's dominion....Because the universal key, the key of God's economy, is in His hand, He opens and shuts. (*The Conclusion of the New Testament,* p. 413)

As the One who has the key of David and who opens and no one will shut, the Lord has given the recovered church an opened door, which no one can shut. Since the recovery of the proper church life began, in the early part of the nineteenth century, until now, a door has always been opened wide to the Lord's recovery.... In spite of much opposition, today the door is open worldwide. The key is in the hand of the Head of the church; it is not in the hand of the opposers. (Rev. 3:8, footnote 1)

The doors are increasingly open to the recovery, and the key is in His hand....Although many opposers rose up against His recovery and tried their best to shut the door, Christ nevertheless is the One who has the key of David. What He opens no one will shut, and what He shuts no one will open. Today we should praise the Lord for the door open worldwide. (*The Conclusion of the New Testament,* p. 4203)

The resurrected Christ in His ascension is seated at the right hand of the Majesty on high (Matt. 22:44; Mark 12:36; Luke 20:42-43; Acts 2:34-35; Heb. 1:13), as the Leader of the universe (Acts 2:36; 5:31; 10:36), having the authority to rule sovereignly over all things. Therefore, the key of David is the key of the kingdom, God's key for ruling the universe. Christ holds the key of David; He has authority to open and shut in order to establish God's kingdom, God's dominion, and to build up God's dwelling, God's temple.

According to Revelation 3 the ascended Christ has the key of David in order to give the church in Philadelphia, a type of the recovered church, an opened door so that people can enter the recovered church to be transformed into pillars in the temple of God and to be built up as God's city, the New Jerusalem (vv. 7-8, 12). (*Truth Lessons—Level Four,* vol. 1, p. 110)

Further Reading: The Conclusion of the New Testament, msgs. 39, 412; *Truth Lessons—Level Four,* vol. 1, lsn. 10

Enlightenment and inspiration: _____

_____

_____

_____

Hymns, #1275

1   Glorious things to thee are spoken,
     Philadelphia, church of love.
  These things saith the One who's holy,
     He who's real speaks from above;
  He that has the key of David,
     Who the kingdom's entrance won,
  "I will open, no man shutteth"—
     He has spoken; it is done.

2   Hallelujah, Philadelphia,
     Thine are works that please the Lord.
  Strength thou hast, though just a little
     And hast kept His living Word.
  Thou His holy name denied not,
     But confessed it here below—
  Lo, a door is set before thee,
     Through which none but thee can go.

3   Thou, beloved Philadelphia,
     Dost His Word of patience keep.
  From the hour of trial He'll save thee,
     Which o'er all the world shall sweep.
  Troublers too shall know He loves thee;
     They to thee must then bow down.
  "Hold thou fast, for I come quickly,
     That no man may take thy crown."

4   Hallelujah, overcomers,
     "In the temple of My God,
  I will build them in as pillars,
     Nevermore to go abroad."
  God's own name is written on them
     And the new name of the Lord.
  With the triune God they're blended;
     They're the city of our God.

5   Hallelujah, out of heaven,
    Comes the New Jerusalem:
    Gates of pearl and walls of jasper,
    Mingled with each precious gem.
    Philadelphia, Philadelphia,
    Has become His Bride so dear.
    Now the Spirit in the churches
    Speaks to all who have an ear.

Composition for prophecy with main point and sub-points: _____

_____

_____

_____

_____

_____

_____

_____

_____

_____

_____

_____

_____

_____

_____

_____

_____

_____

_____

_____

_____

_____

_____

_____

_____

_____

_____

_____

_____

_____

The Greater Jonah

Scripture Reading: Jonah 1:1-2, 17; 2:10; 3:2; 4:11; Matt. 12:38-41

Day 1

I. **As a prophet, Jonah is a type of Christ, the greater Jonah, in His death, burial, and resurrection (Jonah 1:17; 2:10; Matt. 12:38-41):**

A. Through His death on the cross Christ nullified death and destroyed the devil, who has the might of death (2 Tim. 1:10; Heb. 2:14):

1. Christ nullified death, bringing it to naught, doing away with it, abolishing it, annulling it (2 Tim. 1:10).

2. In Genesis 3:15 God promised that the seed of the woman would bruise the head of the serpent; in the fullness of the time the Son of God came to become flesh by being born of a virgin so that on the cross He might destroy the devil, bringing him to naught (Rom. 8:3; Gal. 4:4; John 3:14; 12:31).

Day 2

3. In His work on the cross Christ caused the rulers and the authorities to be stripped off, to be made a display of openly, and to be triumphed over in the cross by God (Col. 2:15).

4. Matthew 27:51-53 describes the effectiveness of the Lord's devil-destroying crucifixion:

a. "The veil of the temple was split in two from top to bottom" (v. 51a); this signifies that the separation between God and man has been abolished because the flesh of sin (the flesh being signified by the veil) taken by Christ in its likeness (Rom. 8:3) has been crucified (Heb. 10:20).

b. "The earth was shaken" (Matt. 27:51b); this signifies that the base of Satan's rebellion was shaken.

c. "The rocks were split" (v. 51c); this signifies that the strongholds of Satan's earthly kingdom were broken.

d. "The tombs were opened" (v. 52a); this signifies that the power of death and Hades
was conquered and subdued.

e. "Many bodies of the saints who had fallen
asleep were raised" (v. 52b); this signifies
the releasing power of the death of Christ.

B. After Christ was buried, He went in the Spirit as
His divinity to the spirits in prison (the rebellious
angels) to proclaim God's victory, through His
incarnation in Christ and Christ's death in the
flesh, over Satan's scheme to derange the divine
plan (1 Pet. 3:18-19; Matt. 12:40; Eph. 4:9):

1. While the Lord Jesus was being put to death in
the flesh, His Spirit as His divinity was made
alive, enlivened, with new power of life, so that
in this empowered Spirit He made proclamation to the fallen angels after His death and
before His resurrection (1 Pet. 3:18-19).

2. Christ proclaimed the victory achieved by
God, that is, that through Christ's death on
the cross God destroyed Satan and his power
of darkness (John 12:31; Col. 2:15; Heb. 2:14).

Day 3 A C. The resurrected Christ is the living One; He is
"living forever and ever" and has "the keys of
death and of Hades" (Rev. 1:18):

1. The Lord Jesus entered into death, but death
could not hold Him, because He is the resurrection; Christ died, but in resurrection He,
the living One, will exist forever and ever
(Acts 2:24; John 11:25).

2. Christ's resurrection was His victory over
death, Satan, Hades, and the grave, and the
keys of death and of Hades are now in His
hand; death is subject to Him, and Hades is
under His control (Rev. 1:18).

3. In the church life today we are no longer subject to death and Hades, for Christ nullified
death on the cross and overcame Hades in

His resurrection (2 Tim. 1:10; Acts 2:24).

Day 4
&   ᗯ
Day 5

    D. The unique sign given by God is "the sign of Jonah the prophet"—the sign of the crucified and resurrected Christ (Matt. 12:38-41):

        1. After the prophet Jonah was in the belly of the great fish for three days, he came out to become a sign to that generation for repentance (Jonah 1:2, 17; 3:2-10).

        2. Jonah is a type of Christ, who would turn from Israel to the Gentiles and who would be buried in the heart of the earth for three days and three nights and then be resurrected, becoming a sign to this generation for salvation (Matt. 12:40-41).

        3. As the One greater than Jonah, Christ in resurrection is the unique sign for today (vv. 38-41).

II. Jonah is a type of Christ announcing the gospel of peace (Jonah 1:1-2; 3:2):

    A. In Hebrew the name Jonah means "dove," indicating that God wanted Jonah to go out like a dove to preach the gospel of peace; thus, Jonah typifies Christ preaching the gospel of peace to the Gentiles (Matt. 12:41).

    B. Christ Himself is peace, on the cross Christ made peace, and in resurrection Christ came to announce peace as the gospel (Eph. 2:13-17).

Day 6

    C. Christ came forth from Hades in resurrection, and in resurrection He became the life-giving Spirit for the preaching, the spreading, of the gospel to all the Gentile nations, as seen in the book of Acts (2:27a; Eph. 4:9; 1 Cor. 15:45b).

    D. In His resurrection Christ, as the greater Jonah, prepared and charged His disciples to preach the gospel and disciple the nations for His propagation so that the church may be produced (Matt. 28:18-19; Mark 16:15; Luke 24:46-48).

III. The book of Jonah indicates particularly that God is not the God only of a certain people; He is the God of all peoples (1:2; 4:11; Rom. 3:29):

A. The Jews thought that they were the unique people of God; they considered themselves the firstborn son with the right to be the first to enjoy all that is of God (Exo. 4:22; Luke 15:11-32).

B. Because the Jews responded to God wrongly, the Gentiles, not the Jews, became the first to enjoy God in His salvation (Matt. 21:18-32; Acts 13:45-48; Rom. 11:11, 17, 25).

C. The book of Jonah indicates that while God was angry with Assyria, He would still be gracious and compassionate toward a great and sinful city such as Nineveh (1:1-2; 4:11).

D. God's economy is to do things through Israel, His suffering people, and the nations, the consuming "locusts" (Joel 1:4), to extend His salvation to all the peoples on earth (Matt. 28:19; Acts 1:8; John 3:16; Rev. 22:17).

a sign to this generation
for salvation.

gospel of peace
to one glory.

Morning Nourishment

Heb. **Since therefore the children have shared in blood**
2:14 **and flesh, He also Himself in like manner partook**
of the same, that through death He might destroy
him who has the might of death, that is, the devil.
2 Tim. **...Our Savior Christ Jesus, who nullified death and**
1:10 **brought life and incorruption to light through the**
gospel.

In Matthew 12:38-41 Christ is unveiled as the One greater
than Jonah. When the scribes and Pharisees asked for a sign, the
Lord Jesus said that no sign would be given "except the sign of
Jonah the prophet" (v. 39). As a prophet, Jonah is a type of Christ
in His death, burial, and resurrection. (*The Conclusion of the New
Testament,* p. 2799)

Today's Reading

Since the Lord destroyed the devil, who has the might of
death, we who were held in slavery through the fear of death
have been released by Him. Death reigned over us (Rom. 5:14),
and we were under its slavery, continually fearing death. Since
the Lord destroyed the devil and nullified death (2 Tim. 1:10), we
now have no more fear of death and are released from its slavery.
(Heb. 2:15, footnote 1)

Due to the sin of Adam, the head of the old creation, everything is under death. In His work on the cross Christ tasted this
death, a death on behalf of everything. This is the reason we say
that Christ's death was an all-inclusive death....In 2 Timothy
1:10 Paul tells us that through His work in His death Christ nullified death. The Greek word translated "nullified" also means
make of none effect, bring to naught, do away with, abolish,
annul, discard. Through His devil-destroying death, Christ nullified death, making it of none effect. To nullify death does not
mean to remove death but to make it of no effect. Death will
not be removed until it is cast into the lake of fire after the millennium (Rev. 20:14). Death will be the last enemy destroyed by

the Lord (1 Cor. 15:26). Although death has not yet been removed, it is nonetheless a fact that it has been nullified through
Christ's death on the cross. (*The Conclusion of the New Testament,* pp. 773-774)

The seed of the woman is the incarnated Jesus Christ, who
as the very God was born of the virgin Mary to be a man, as prophesied in Isaiah 7:14, fulfilled in Matthew 1:23, and confirmed in
Galatians 4:4. Thus, the promise here indicates that God Himself
would come to be a human seed to bruise the head of the damaging
serpent. Ultimately, the seed of the woman is enlarged to include
the overcoming believers, the stronger part of God's people, signified by the man-child in Revelation 12:5 (see footnote 2 there). The
man-child, the corporate seed of the woman, includes the Lord Jesus, the individual seed of the woman. Psalm 2:8-9, Revelation
2:26-27, and Revelation 12:5 indicate that the Lord Jesus as God's
Anointed, the overcomers in the churches, and the man-child will
rule the nations with an iron rod, thus proving that the Lord Jesus,
the overcomers, and the man-child are one. The Lord as the leading
Overcomer (Rev. 3:21) is the Head, center, reality, life, and nature of
the man-child, and the man-child as the following overcomers is
the Lord's Body. (Gen. 3:15, footnote 3)

The bruising of the serpent's head by the seed of the woman
is the destroying of Satan, the one who has the might of death,
by the Lord Jesus through His death on the cross (Heb. 2:14 and
footnote; 1 John 3:8). While the Lord was destroying the serpent
on the cross, the serpent bruised His heel, that is, wounded Him
by nailing His feet to the cross (Psa. 22:16).

Through the Lord's death on the cross, Satan, the old serpent,
was judged, cast out (John 12:31; 16:11). That judgment will ultimately be carried out by the overcomers as the man-child, the
corporate seed of the woman (Rev. 12:9 and footnote 1). (Gen.
3:15, footnote 4)

Further Reading: The Conclusion of the New Testament, msg. 270;
Life-study of Genesis, msgs. 19-20

Enlightenment and inspiration: _____

_____

_____

_____

Morning Nourishment

Col.   Stripping off the rulers and the authorities, He made
2:15   a display *of them* openly, triumphing over them in it.
1 Pet. For Christ also has suffered once for sins...on the
3:18-19 one hand being put to death in the flesh, but on the
        other, made alive in the Spirit; in which also He
        went and proclaimed to the spirits in prison.

[In Colossians 2:15] we see that in His work on the cross
Christ caused the rulers and authorities to be stripped off, to be
made a display of openly, and to be triumphed over in the cross
by God. The rulers and authorities spoken of in this verse are
the angelic rulers and authorities. The Greek word for "stripping off" can also be rendered "putting off." The Greek word for
"make a display" means show or exhibit in the sense of putting
to an open shame. God openly shamed the evil angelic rulers
and authorities on the cross and triumphed over them in it. (*The
Conclusion of the New Testament,* p. 774)

Today's Reading

[Matthew 27:51-56] reveals the effect of Christ's crucifixion.
Verse 51 says, "And behold, the veil of the temple was split in two
from top to bottom." This signifies that the separation between God
and man was abolished, because the flesh (signified by the veil) of
sin taken by Christ (Rom. 8:3) had been crucified (Heb. 10:20). The
words "from top to bottom" indicate that the rending of the veil was
God's doing from above. Because sin had been judged and the flesh
of sin had been crucified, the separation between God and man was
taken away. Now the way to enter into the presence of God is open
for us. What a wonderful effect of the Lord's death! His death was
not martyrdom; it was an act of redemption....Matthew 27:51 also
says that "the earth was shaken and the rocks were split." The
shaking of the earth signifies that the base of Satan's rebellion has
been shaken, and the splitting of the rocks signifies that the
strongholds of Satan's earthly kingdom have been broken. Hallelujah, the Lord's death tore the veil, shook the base of Satan's rebellion, and broke the strongholds of Satan's kingdom! What a death!

Praise the Lord for His death! Because God's righteousness was fully satisfied, Christ's death could be so effective....Verses 52 and 53 say, "And the tombs were opened, and many bodies of the saints who had fallen asleep were raised. And they came out of the tombs after His resurrection and entered into the holy city and appeared to many." The opening of the tombs signifies that the power of death and Hades has been conquered and subdued, and the raising of the bodies of the saints signifies the releasing power of the death of Christ. (*Life-study of Matthew*, pp. 812-813)

[*The Spirit* in 1 Peter 3:18 refers] not [to] the Holy Spirit, but [to] the Spirit [as the essence of Christ's divinity (Rom. 1:4; cf. John 4:24a)].... The crucifixion only put Christ to death in His flesh, which He received through His incarnation (John 1:14), not in His Spirit [as His divinity]. His Spirit did not die at the cross when His flesh did. His Spirit was rather made alive, enlivened, with new power of life, so that in this empowered Spirit He made a proclamation to the fallen angels after His death in the flesh and before His resurrection.

After His death in the flesh, Christ in His living Spirit went (probably to the abyss—Rom. 10:7) to these rebellious angels to proclaim, perhaps, God's victory through His incarnation in Christ and Christ's death in the flesh, over Satan's scheme to derange the divine plan.

Christ did not preach the gospel to the spirits in prison; He made a proclamation to them. He proclaimed to those rebellious angels God's victory over Satan through Christ's incarnation and death. At that time, Christ had not yet been resurrected. It was after His death that He went to that particular place, in His empowered Spirit, to proclaim Christ's victory. Perhaps He said, "You angels followed Satan to rebel against God. But through My incarnation and death, your leader, Satan, has been conquered." This proclamation is a shame to Satan and his followers, but it is a glory to God. (*Life-study of 1 Peter*, pp. 217-219)

Further Reading: The Conclusion of the New Testament, msg. 72; *Life-study of 1 Peter*, msg. 24

Enlightenment and inspiration: _____

_____

_____

_____

Morning Nourishment

Acts **Whom God has raised up, having loosed the pangs**
2:24 **of death, since it was not possible for Him to be**
held by it.
Rev. **And the living One; and I became dead, and behold,**
1:18 **I am living forever and ever; and I have the keys of**
death and of Hades.

In Revelation 1:18 we see that the Lord is "the living One," the
One who "became dead" and who is "living forever and ever."
The Lord suffered death and lived again. He entered into death,
but death could not hold Him (Acts 2:24), because He is the resurrection (John 11:25). Christ died, but in resurrection He will live
forever. Resurrection is the lengthening of the Lord's days. He will
exist forever and ever in His resurrection. Jesus Christ today is
the living One, the One who is in resurrection. For Christ to dispense life, He must be the living One since a dead person can
never dispense life to others.

The importance of His being the living One is that He is living in us. He is living forever and is living in us. (*The Conclusion
of the New Testament*, p. 4153)

Today's Reading

[The Lord] wants us to leave every kind of death and rise up to
be the living church. The living One within us can never be dead.
His church should be neither dead nor deadened; instead, His
church must be living all the time. We must learn to enjoy Christ as
the living One. His living forever is His testimony, for the testimony
of Jesus is always related to the matter of being living. If a local
church is not living, it will not have the testimony of Jesus. The more
living we are, the more we are the testimony of the living Jesus.

We have a living Christ who has overcome death. Our Christ,
who is the resurrected One, is living in us and among us. He is living forever and ever. What a living Christ we have in the recovery!
In the recovery all the churches should be as living as Christ, full
of life and overcoming death.

In Revelation 1:18 the Lord also says, "I have the keys of death and of Hades." Due to the fall and sin of man, death came in and is now working on earth to gather up all the sinful people into Hades. Death resembles a dustpan used to collect the dust from the floor, and Hades resembles a trash can. Whatever the dustpan collects is put into the trash can. Thus, death is a collector, and Hades is a keeper. In the church life today we are no longer subject to death and Hades, for Christ abolished death on the cross and overcame Hades in His resurrection. Although Hades tried its best to hold Him, it was powerless to do it (Acts 2:24). With Him, death has no sting and Hades has no power. We must be the same as Christ. In the church life the keys of death and Hades are in His hand. It is impossible for us to deal with death; we simply do not have the ability to handle it. Whenever death enters, it will deaden many. But as long as we give the Lord Jesus the ground, the opportunity, and the free way to move and act among us, both death and Hades will be under His control. However, whenever the Lord Jesus does not have the ground in the church, death immediately becomes prevailing and Hades becomes powerful to hold the dead ones. We should praise the Lord that Christ has the keys of death and of Hades. Death is subject to Him, and Hades is under His control.

Christ's resurrection was also His victory over death, Satan, Hades, and the grave (2:24)....Christ, the Son of Man, was not only vindicated by God and was proved to be a success in His achievements, but He was victorious over death, Satan, Hades, and the grave, all of which are a great concern and trouble to us. The Son of Man overcame death and destroyed Satan (Heb. 2:14). The keys of death and of Hades are now in His hand (Rev. 1:18), and He is victorious over the grave. Such a Christ is walking in the midst of all the local churches in His recovery, taking care of them as the golden lampstands. (*The Conclusion of the New Testament,* pp. 4153-4156)

Further Reading: The Conclusion of the New Testament, msgs. 364, 407

Enlightenment and inspiration: _____

_____

_____

_____

Morning Nourishment

Matt. But He answered and said to them, An evil and
12:39 adulterous generation seeks after a sign, and a sign
     shall not be given to it except the sign of Jonah the
     prophet.
  41 Ninevite men will stand up in the judgment with
     this generation and will condemn it, because they
     repented at the preaching of Jonah, and behold,
     something more than Jonah is here.

Because the Pharisees could not argue with the Lord Jesus,
they changed the subject seemingly from the negative side to
the positive side. Matthew 12:38 says, "Then some of the scribes
and Pharisees answered Him, saying, Teacher, we want to see a
sign from You." Because they could not defeat the Lord Jesus by
arguing, to save face they changed the subject from one thing to
another; they asked the Lord for a sign. This was a subtle pro-
posal. A sign is a miracle with some spiritual significance. The
Jews always seek for signs (1 Cor. 1:22). Once again this gave
the Lord the opportunity to reveal to the whole universe something further concerning Himself. (*Life-study of Matthew*, p. 417)

Today's Reading

If you had been one of those Pharisees, would you not have
been bothered by the Lord's reply [in Matthew 12:39]? The
Pharisees seemed to be saying, "We want you to show us a sign,
and you call us an evil and adulterous generation. Before this,
you called us a brood of vipers. We recognize that you are a good
teacher. Teacher, show us a sign. Show us a miracle with some
significance." The Lord Jesus seemed to say, "Yes, you will see a
sign. Although you are not an honest generation nor a pure generation, but an evil and adulterous generation, there is a sign for
you—the sign of Jonah."

The Lord Jesus proceeded to tell them the significance of the sign
of Jonah. In verse 40 He said, "For just as Jonah was in the belly of
the great fish three days and three nights, so will the Son of Man
be in the heart of the earth three days and three nights." This was

to be a very meaningful sign to them. "The heart of the earth" is called the lower parts of the earth (Eph. 4:9) and Hades (Acts 2:27), where the Lord went after His death. Hades, equal to Sheol in the Old Testament, has two sections: the section of torment and the section of comfort (Luke 16:23-26). The section of comfort is paradise, where the Lord went with the saved thief after they died (Luke 23:43). Hence, the heart of the earth, the lower parts of the earth, Hades, and paradise are synonymous terms, referring to the one place where the Lord stayed for three days and three nights after His death and before His resurrection.

In Matthew 12:41 the Lord continued, "Ninevite men will stand up in the judgment with this generation and will condemn it, because they repented at the preaching of Jonah, and behold, something more than Jonah is here." The Greek word rendered *more* in verses 41 and 42 is *pleion,* meaning better in quality and larger in quantity; hence, more. It differs from *meizon,* the word for *greater* in verse 6, which means greater in external size or measure.... [Christ was] buried in the heart of the earth for three days and then [He] resurrected, becoming a sign to this generation for salvation.

In verse 41 the Lord seemed to be saying, "The Ninevites repented because of the sign of Jonah. Yet you, an evil and adulterous generation, which will see such a sign as that of the Son of Man buried in the heart of the earth for three days and three nights, will not repent." The Lord's word in verses 40 and 41 was not an ordinary word; it was a prediction. Before the Lord was buried in the heart of the earth, He prophesied in this way, telling the Pharisees that He would be three days and three nights in the heart of the earth. I believe that the Lord Jesus told them this in His mercy. He seemed to say, "I give you a prediction of My death and burial. This shall be a sign to you, just as Jonah was a sign to the Ninevites that caused them all to repent. I predict this now so that when you see it, you may repent." (*Life-study of Matthew,* pp. 417-419)

Further Reading: Life-study of Matthew, msg. 34; *Christ versus Religion,* ch. 3

Enlightenment and inspiration: _____

_____

_____

_____

Morning Nourishment

Eph. **Abolishing in His flesh the law of the command-**
2:15 **ments in ordinances, that He might create the two**
      in Himself into one new man, *so* making peace.
   17 And coming, He announced peace as the gospel to you
      who were far off, and peace to those who were near.

[In Matthew 12] the religious people came to the Lord Jesus asking for a sign, a miracle. They wanted Him to perform a miracle to prove that He was of God. He answered them in this way: "An evil and adulterous generation seeks after a sign, and a sign shall not be given to it except the sign of Jonah the prophet" (12:39). Jonah was a prophet who spent three days and three nights buried within a great fish in the waters of death. After three days he came out. This was a type of the crucifixion and resurrection of the Lord Jesus. The Lord Jesus indicated to the religious people that their generation would see no sign except the unique sign of the crucified and resurrected Christ....The sign that is needed today is not a wonder or a miracle; it is the sign of a crucified and resurrected person. (*The Kingdom,* p. 227)

Today's Reading

As the One greater than Jonah, Christ preaches glad tidings to the nations....[In Matthew 12:41] we see that Christ, as the Prophet sent by God to His people (Deut. 18:15, 18), is greater than Jonah the prophet. Jonah turned from Israel to the Gentiles and was put into the belly of the great fish. After he had remained there for three days and three nights, he came out to be a sign to that generation for repentance (Jonah 1:2, 17; 3:2-10). This was a type of Christ, who would turn from Israel to the Gentiles....As the One greater than Jonah, Christ in resurrection is the unique sign for today. (*The Conclusion of the New Testament,* p. 2800)

Among the books of the Minor Prophets, Jonah stands alone....Jonah 1:1-2 is the introductory word to this book....Jonah in Hebrew means "dove" (v. 1). This signifies that God wanted Jonah to go out as a dove to preach the gospel of peace.

The central thought of the book of Jonah is that God cared for

and saved even the most evil Gentiles in His pity on men and cattle....In the book of Jonah, the revelation concerning Christ is in
Jonah's being a type of Christ....Christ is revealed in Jonah's typifying Christ preaching the gospel of peace to the Gentiles (3:2;
Matt. 12:41). Jonah was a prophet who turned from Israel to the
Gentiles. In this he was a type of Christ, who turned from Israel to
the Gentiles (Luke 4:25-27; Matt. 21:43). (*Life-study of Jonah*, pp. 1-2)

Speaking of Christ, [Ephesians] 2:14 says, "He Himself is our
peace." The word *our* refers to both Jewish and Gentile believers.
Through the blood of Christ we have been brought near both to
God and to God's people. Christ, who has accomplished full
redemption for both Jewish and Gentile believers, is Himself our
peace, our harmony, in that He made both one. Due to the fall of
mankind and the call of the chosen race, there was a separation
between Israel and the Gentiles. Through Christ's redemption,
this separation has been removed. Now the two are one in the
redeeming Christ, who is the bond of oneness.

At present, there is still a separation between Israel and the
rest of mankind. But according to God's economy, this separation
has already been removed. In the eyes of God, it was taken away
by the redemption of Christ on the cross. Now the Christ who has
removed this separation is the bond of peace between Israel and
the Gentiles. (*Life-study of Ephesians*, p. 197)

God created man as a collective entity (Gen. 1:26). The corporate man created by God was damaged through man's fall; hence,
there was the need for God to produce a new man. This was
accomplished through Christ's abolishing in His flesh the ordinances and through His creating of the new man in Himself....By
Christ's abolishing in His flesh the separating ordinances, that is,
His slaying the enmity, and by His creating the Jewish and the
Gentile believers into one new man, peace was made between all
believers. (Eph. 2:15, footnotes 8 and 9)

Further Reading: The Kingdom, ch. 23: Life-study of Ephesians,
    msgs. 22-24

Enlightenment and inspiration: _bond of peace_

Morning Nourishment

Jonah   And I, should I not have pity on Nineveh, the great
4:11   city, in which are more than a hundred and twenty
        thousand people who cannot discern between their
        right hand and their left, and many cattle?
Acts   ...You shall be My witnesses both in Jerusalem and
1:8   in all Judea and Samaria and unto the uttermost
        part of the earth.

Christ is revealed also in the type of Jonah's staying in the
great fish three days and three nights (Jonah 1:17). This typifies
Christ's staying in the heart of the earth three days and three
nights (Matt. 12:40). Christ died and entered into the heart of the
earth. He came forth from there in resurrection, and in resurrection He became the life-giving Spirit (1 Cor. 15:45b) for the
preaching, the spreading, of the gospel to all the Gentile nations,
as seen in the book of Acts.

As we have pointed out, Jonah here was a type of Christ, who
was sent by God to preach the gospel to the Gentiles, with Jonah's
staying in the great fish three days and three nights typifying
Christ's staying in the heart of the earth three days and three
nights. (*Life-study of Jonah,* pp. 2-3)

Today's Reading

In His work in His resurrection Christ prepared and charged
the disciples to preach the gospel and disciple the nations for His
propagation that the church may be produced. Luke 24:44 and 45
say, "...All the things written in the Law of Moses and the Prophets and Psalms concerning Me must be fulfilled...." The Law of
Moses, the Prophets, and Psalms are the three sections of the
entire Old Testament, that is, all the Scriptures (v. 27). The Lord's
word here unveils that the entire Old Testament was a revelation
of Him and that He was its center and content. (*The Conclusion of
the New Testament,* p. 804)

In Jonah 4:11 we see God's pity on the most evil city of the
Gentiles; He cared even for their cattle. Nineveh was built by
the evil man Nimrod in Assyria (Gen. 10:8-11). Assyria was the

country that invaded and insulted Israel about 713 B.C. (Isa. 36), after the time of Jonah. God had pity on such an evil city.

In Matthew 12:40 the Lord Jesus told the Pharisees, a group of "Jonahs," that He would be in the heart of the earth three days and three nights, just as Jonah was in the belly of the great fish, for the extending of God's salvation from the Jews to the Gentiles. This indicates that God is not only the God of the Jews but also the God of all the nations. The Jews thought that they were the unique people of God. They considered themselves the firstborn son (Luke 15:25-32) with the right to be the first to enjoy all that is of God. But because the Jews responded to God wrongly, the Gentiles, not the Jews, became the first to enjoy God in His salvation.

The book of Jonah indicates particularly that God...is the God of all peoples. After Christ's resurrection and ascension and the outpouring of the Holy Spirit, in Acts 13 God told Paul and Barnabas to go to the Gentiles (vv. 46-47). They were not like Jonah; rather, they took God's commission and went and preached the gospel throughout Asia Minor. Then the Spirit led them to go from Asia to Europe, to Macedonia (16:6-10). The book of Jonah shows us that while God was angry with Assyria, He would still be gracious and compassionate toward a great and sinful city such as Nineveh. This indicates that God's economy is to do things through these two factors—the consuming factor and the suffering factor—to extend His salvation to all the peoples on earth.

God's economy to manifest Christ implies the extending of His salvation in Christ to reach even the distant, great, evil cities of the Gentiles. I consider Russia as today's Nineveh. What we are doing in Russia is altogether under the span of God's economy. I believe that we will receive much blessing because this is according to God's economy. Thus, the consuming locusts are still consuming, the suffering Israel is still suffering, and the Lord is still going on in His recovery. (*Life-study of Jonah*, pp. 6-7)

Further Reading: Life-study of Jonah, msg. 1; The Conclusion of the New Testament, msg. 74

Enlightenment and inspiration: _____

_____

_____

_____

Hymns, #62

1   Dear Lord Jesus, we adore Thee,
      "Seed of woman" Thou became;
  Of the virgin wast begotten,
      Called e'en with a human name.
  Taking thus the human nature,
      Thou as man the serpent trod;
  By the Cross his head Thou bruisèd
  And fulfilled the plan of God.

      Lord, we see Thy glory,
      Shown in human beauty,
      Full of splendor, manifested
        In humanity.

2   As a man, by incarnation,
      Flesh and blood didst Thou partake
  To destroy the devil, Satan,
      In our stead and for our sake.
  With the name of Jesus given
      And Emmanuel callèd too,
  Thou becam'st our precious Savior,
      Bringing us salvation true.

3   Thou, "Last Adam" wast entitled,
      And wast called the "second man",
  Head of all the new creation,
      Better than the first man.
  On this earth in life and conduct
      Thou indeed wast Son of man;
  Now in heaven with this nature
      Thou dost still appear as man.

4   In the time which God appointed
      Thou wilt come, dear Lord, again,
  With the glory of the Father,
      Still appearing as a man.
  Even on the throne of judgment
      Son of man Thou still wilt be;
  And with this, our human nature,
      Thou forevermore wilt be.

Composition for prophecy with main point and sub-points: _____

_____

_____

_____

_____

_____

_____

_____

_____

_____

_____

_____

_____

_____

_____

_____

_____

_____

_____

_____

_____

_____

_____

_____

_____

_____

_____

_____

_____

_____

_____

_____

_____

_____

_____

_____

Christ's "Goings Forth"
from the Days of Eternity

Scripture Reading: Micah 5:2-5a; John 1:1, 3, 14, 29, 32-42, 51

Day 1 I. **"You, O Bethlehem Ephrathah, / So little to be among the thousands of Judah, / From you there will come forth to Me / He who is to be Ruler in Israel; / And His goings forth are from ancient times, / From the days of eternity"** **(Micah 5:2):**

A. This verse prophesies concerning the incarnation of Christ in Bethlehem (Matt. 2:4-6; Luke 2:4-7).

B. Although Christ came forth from Bethlehem, His goings forth were from ancient times, from the days of eternity; this refers to Christ's eternal origin and indicates that in eternity, before the creation of the earth, Christ was preparing to come forth.

C. Christ's appearing, His manifestation, began in eternity; from ancient times, from the days of eternity, the Triune God was preparing to come forth out of eternity into time, to come with His divinity into humanity by being born in Bethlehem as a man.

D. His creating of all things was His preparation for Him to come out of eternity into time; this was the purpose of creation.

E. Then, while the "locusts" were operating to consume Israel (Joel 1:4; 2:25), Christ came forth.

F. Christ's going forth, His appearing, is a continuous matter:

1. At the time of His incarnation He began to come forth.

2. He continued to go forth through His human living, His death, His resurrection, His ascension, His outpouring of the consummated Spirit (who is the reality of Christ Himself), and His spreading through the preaching of the gospel

to the whole inhabited earth; all these are great steps in Christ's going forth.

3. Christ's going forth, His manifestation, will consummate when He comes back to defeat Antichrist and cast him into the lake of fire (Rev. 19:19-20), when Satan is cast into the abyss (20:2-3), and when Christ sets up His throne to reign as King (Matt. 25:31, 34, 40); at that time His appearing will be complete.

G. While Christ is on the way, He is taking care of the scattered Jews; on the one hand, Israel is under God's chastisement; on the other hand, Israel is also under God's shepherding care; this shepherding is God's preservation of Israel.

H. In the restoration Christ will be the Ruler, the Shepherd, and the peace to His elect, Israel (Micah 5:2-5a); today, as our Ruler, Christ keeps us; as our Shepherd, He nourishes and cherishes us; and as our peace, He controls our environment so that we may enjoy Him.

Day 2
&
Day 3

II. Christ's goings forth from the days of eternity are also seen in the first chapter of the Gospel of John, which unveils Christ as the Word of God in the two sections of eternity with the bridge of time (cf. Psa. 90:1):

Day 4

A. The Word of God in John 1:1 refers to Christ, the only begotten Son of God (v. 18), in eternity past as the definition, explanation, and expression of God:

1. He is the great "I Am," self-existing and ever-existing (Exo. 3:14-15; John 8:24, 28, 58).

2. He is eternal, without beginning or ending (Heb. 7:3).

B. John 1 is the introduction to the whole Gospel of John, and the main stress of this introduction is that Christ is the Word of God—the definition, explanation, and expression of the mysterious and invisible God; it refers to Christ and His goings forth from the days of eternity in the five greatest events in the history of the universe:

1. John 1 reveals Christ in the creation of all things in the beginning of time (v. 3).
2. Christ is also seen in the incarnation of the invisible God to be a visible man (v. 14), partaking of man's flesh and blood (Heb. 2:14), for the redemption of the lost universe to bring in the New Testament age.
3. Christ is also revealed in His becoming the Lamb to take away the sin of the world (mankind) judicially for the New Testament (John 1:29, 36):
   a. Christ was "delivered up by the determined counsel and foreknowledge of God" (Acts 2:23a).
   b. This counsel must have been determined in a council held by the Divine Trinity before the foundation of the world, indicating that the Lord's crucifixion was not an accident in human history but a purposeful fulfillment of the divine counsel determined by the Triune God (1 Pet. 1:20; Rev. 13:8).
   c. The redeeming Christ was "foreknown before the foundation of the world" (1 Pet. 1:20).
   d. Christ was crucified on the cross for our judicial redemption according to God's eternal purpose and plan; it did not happen accidentally.
   e. Hence, in the eternal view of God, from the foundation of the world, that is, from the fall of man as part of the world, Christ was slain (Rev. 13:8).

Day 5

4. Christ is revealed in His becoming the Spirit for the transformation of God's redeemed people into stones (John 1:32-42) for the building of God's house (Bethel—v. 51) organically for the New Testament.
5. Finally, Christ is referred to in His being the heavenly ladder to bring heaven to earth and join earth to heaven at Bethel, the house of God, from His coming back to eternity future (v. 51; Gen. 28:11-22).

      6. These five great historical events, which include Christ's goings forth from the days of eternity, can be summed up in five words: *creation, incarnation, Lamb, Spirit,* and *ladder.*

  C. In all these five universal, historical events, Christ, the Word of God (as: 1. the Creator in creation; 2. the man in incarnation; 3. the Lamb in redemption; 4. the Spirit in transformation; and 5. the ladder in joining earth to heaven), defines, explains, and expresses the invisible God:

      1. In His creation "the heavens are telling of the glory of God; / And their expanse [firmament] is declaring the work of His hands. / Day to day pours forth speech, / And night to night reveals knowledge. / There is no speech, nor are there words; / Their voice is not heard" (Psa. 19:1-3, NASB), and the invisible things of God, "both His eternal power and divine characteristics, have been clearly seen since the creation of the world" (Rom. 1:20); what is referred to in Acts 14:15-17 and 17:24-29 serves the same purpose of revealing Christ's creation.

      2. In His incarnation He unveils that the Creator has become one of His creatures (Col. 1:15), bringing God into man, mingling divinity with humanity as one, and in His human living He expresses God in the divine attributes through His human virtues.

Day 6

      3. In His becoming the Lamb for the redemption of the lost world, Christ speaks to us how God accomplished His redemption judicially through His death as the procedure according to His righteousness.

      4. In His becoming the Spirit for life-giving and transforming (1 Cor. 15:45), Christ speaks to us further how God carries out His economy organically by His divine life for His divine purpose according to His heart's desire.

      5. Christ, in His being the heavenly ladder at

Bethel, also speaks to us how God desires to have a house on the earth constituted with His redeemed and transformed elect, that He may bring heaven to earth and join earth to heaven, to make the two as one for eternity.

6. In addition to all the above items, John, in his last writing, Revelation, tells us that even in the warfare for the kingdom of God, Christ is the Word of God speaking for God's purpose (19:13).

D. Christ's goings forth from the days of eternity usher in God's eternal building, the New Jerusalem, which will be the ultimate fulfillment of God's eternal plan as the mutual abode of God and man (21:3, 22; cf. Psa. 90:1):

1. By Christ's goings forth from the days of eternity, Christ as the Word of God in eternity past becomes (united, mingled, and incorporated with His chosen ones) the New Jerusalem in eternity future.

2. This eternal building, the New Jerusalem, will terminate the bridge of time and usher in the blessed eternity in the future (cf. Eccl. 3:11).

3. We must be for that building, and we must be that building (John 1:51; Gen. 28:11-22; 1 Cor. 3:9, 12a, 16-17).

Morning Nourishment

Matt. ...[Herod] inquired of them where the Christ was
2:4-5 to be born. And they said to him, In Bethlehem of
       Judea, for so it is written through the prophet.
Micah (But you, O Bethlehem Ephrathah, so little to be
5:2   among the thousands of Judah, from you there
       will come forth to Me He who is to be Ruler in
       Israel; and His goings forth are from ancient times,
       from the days of eternity.)

His "goings forth" [in Micah 5:2] are His coming out . To the angels it is His going forth, but to us it is His coming out. "His goings
forth are...from the days of eternity" means that in eternity, before
the creation of the earth, Christ was preparing to come forth....
From the ancient times, from the days of eternity, the Triune God
was preparing to come forth out of eternity into time, to come with
His divinity into humanity. His creation of all things was His preparation to come out of eternity into time. This was the purpose of
creation....In eternity Christ was concealed in His divinity, but
through incarnation He came forth with His divinity into humanity. (*Life-study of Micah*, p. 9)

Today's Reading

Christ's going forth, His appearing, is a continuous matter.
From the time of His incarnation, He began to come forth, and
His coming forth is still taking place today. Christ's coming forth
will be consummated when He throws Antichrist and the false
prophet into the lake of fire (Rev. 19:19-20), when Satan is cast
into the abyss (Rev. 20:2-3), and when Christ sets up His throne to
reign as King (Matt. 25:31, 34, 40). At that time His appearing
will be complete. But today He is still on the way.

In the restoration Christ will be the Ruler, Shepherd, and
peace to His elect, Israel (Micah 5:2-5a). Today, in His goings forth,
He is our Ruler, Shepherd, and peace. As our Ruler, He keeps us;
as our Shepherd, He nourishes and cherishes us; and as our
peace, He controls our environment so that we may enjoy Him.

Micah's prophecy concerning the goings forth of the all-inclusive Christ is a great matter. In this prophecy Christ is all-inclusive because He will be the Ruler, the Shepherd, and the peace of Israel, and He will also bring forth the seven shepherds and the eight princes (5:2-5). Christ came forth from Bethlehem, a small town called "David's city" (Luke 2:4). However, His goings forth were not from time but from eternity. In eternity past He selected us and predestinated us (Eph. 1:4-5). When He was doing these things, He considered how He would come. If He had only selected and predestinated us without preparing to come out of eternity, He could do nothing with us. Whatever He will do and can do for us depends on His coming forth. He came in incarnation, and He went on through human living, death, resurrection, ascension, and the outpouring of the consummated Spirit, who is the reality of Christ Himself. All these are great steps in Christ's going forth. His going forth has not stopped but is continuing today. (*Life-study of Micah,* pp. 9, 16)

At the time of His incarnation [Christ] began to come forth. After His incarnation, He continued to go forth through His human living, His death, His resurrection, His ascension, His outpouring of the consummated Spirit (who is the reality of Christ Himself), and His spreading through the preaching of the gospel to the whole inhabited earth. All these are great steps in Christ's going forth. His going forth has not ceased but is continuing today. Christ's going forth, His manifestation, will consummate when He comes back with the overcomers as the mighty ones (Joel 3:11) to defeat Antichrist and cast him into the lake of fire (Rev. 19:19-20), when Satan is cast into the abyss (Rev. 20:2-3), and when Christ sets up His throne to reign as King (Matt. 25:31, 34, 40).

While Christ is on the way, He is taking care of the scattered Jews. On the one hand, Israel is under God's chastisement; on the other hand, Israel is also under God's shepherding care. This shepherding is God's preservation of Israel. (Micah 5:2, footnote 1)

Further Reading: Life-study of Micah, msgs. 2-3

Enlightenment and inspiration: _____

_____

_____

_____

Morning Nourishment

John In the beginning was the Word, and the Word was
1:1   with God, and the Word was God.
51   And He said to him, Truly, truly, I say to you, You
      shall see heaven opened and the angels of God as-
      cending and descending on the Son of Man.

John 1 reveals the two sections of eternity. John 1:1 refers to
eternity in the past, for "the beginning" denotes eternity in the
past. Verse 51 refers to eternity in the future, for when the Lord
told Nathanael that he would see the heaven opened and the
angels of God ascending and descending on the Son of Man, He
was not speaking about the present, but about eternity in the
future. If we put together these two sections of eternity, we have
the whole of eternity. (*Life-study of John,* p. 55)

Today's Reading

In eternity past, Christ, as the Word, was with God and was
God. In eternity past He was only God and only had divinity.
Since the Word had not yet been incarnated, He was not a man
and had no humanity.

In eternity future, Christ will not only be God, but also man.
He will not only be the Son of God, but also the Son of Man. Since
the Word has been incarnated in the flesh (John 1:14), He is also
a man, the Son of Man with humanity forever. After the incarnation, He is still God, but God and man. He is still the Son of God,
but the Son of God and the Son of Man. In addition to being the
Son of God, for eternity in the future He will be the Son of Man. In
eternity past He was God, solely and merely divine, having no
humanity. However, in eternity future He will be God and man,
the Son of God and the Son of Man, both divine and human, having divinity as well as humanity. He will have two natures, two
essences, and two substances—divinity and humanity.

God has no intention of dwelling in Himself. Divinity cannot be
God's dwelling. God's intention in His economy is to dwell in humanity. God's intention is to defeat His enemy, Satan, by man and
to make humanity His dwelling place. Thus, both for the defeat of

Satan and for the dwelling place of God, there is the need of humanity. If the Lord Jesus were only the Son of God, He would only be qualified to impart life into man. He would have no substance by which to defeat the enemy or to become the dwelling place of God. Praise the Lord that He is the Son of God for us to have life, and He is the Son of Man for God to have a dwelling place.

Heaven is considered as God's habitation (Deut. 26:15; 1 Kings 8:49; Psa. 33:13-14; Isa. 63:15); yet [in Isaiah 66:1] God says, "Where is the place of My rest?" God's resting place is man gained by Him (Isa. 57:15; 66:2). Today God dwells in the heavens, but the heavens will not be His habitation for eternity....In the new heaven and the new earth, God's habitation for eternity will be the New Jerusalem, which is composed of all His redeemed saints and which will come down from heaven (Rev. 21:1-3).

How can God, who had no humanity in eternity past, have humanity in eternity future as His dwelling place? This will not happen overnight. Between these two sections of eternity is the bridge of time. In eternity past God planned and purposed, but He did not do anything. In eternity future God will not do anything, because, at that time, everything will have been accomplished. In eternity future He will simply enjoy His finished work. In eternity past He planned, and in eternity future He will enjoy. Everything that God needs to accomplish He accomplishes on the bridge of time. God is driving the car of His economy from the first section of eternity, through the bridge of time, into the last section of eternity. By driving His car across the bridge of time, all the necessary work is completed. Once God has traveled from eternity past, through the bridge of time, and into eternity future, He will declare, "Finished!" In eternity future God will enjoy His finished work.

How long is this bridge of time? It may be more or less than six thousand years long. On this bridge of time God accomplishes five things, and we need to consider each of them in turn. We begin with creation. (*Life-study of John*, pp. 55-59)

Further Reading: Life-study of John, msg. 5

Enlightenment and inspiration: _____

_____

_____

Morning Nourishment

John **All things came into being through Him, and apart**
1:3 **from Him not one thing came into being which has**
     come into being.
14 **And the Word became flesh and tabernacled among**
     us (and we beheld His glory, <u>glory as of the only</u>
     <u>Begotten from the Father), full of grace and reality.</u>

The meaning of creation is to call things not being as being
(Rom. 4:17). The purpose of creation is to produce a receptacle to receive God as life. Consider the items in creation: the heavens, the
earth, the billions of physical things, and man. What is the most
important item in creation? Nothing is more important than man.
Man is a V.I.P., a very important person. According to the Bible, the
heavens are for the earth, and the earth is for man (Zech. 12:1)....
The minerals, the vegetable life, and the animal life are all for
man. The air, sunshine, and rain supply the vegetable life; the
vegetable life is for the animal life, and both the vegetable life
and the animal life are for man. All the living things on the earth
are for man. Man, for whom all these things are, is for God, receiving God and fulfilling His purpose. There is a spirit within man
which is the very receiver of God. By His creation, God produced
the heavens for the earth, the earth for man, and man with a spirit
as a receiver to receive God as his life. (*Life-study of John*, p. 59)

Today's Reading

The second item [God accomplished on the bridge of time] was
incarnation. Without creation there would have been no way for
God to be incarnated....Creation brought things into being, and
incarnation brought God into His creation. God waited approxi-
mately four thousand years after the creation of Adam before
becoming incarnated. One day, He was incarnated, and there was
on earth the little man Jesus with God in Him. God was wrought
into that man. That was the greatest miracle of all. By incarnation, God was brought into mankind and became one with man.
Divinity and humanity became one unit.

The third item on the bridge of time is redemption. After

living on the earth for thirty-three and a half years, the Lord went to the cross as the Lamb of God. The Lamb of God is for redemption. Through redemption, the Lord recovered fallen man and separated him from sin. By means of redemption, God not only removed sin, but also terminated the entire old creation. The very Jesus who was crucified on the cross took the old creation with Him into the tomb. When He was raised from the dead, He left the old creation in the tomb and came out in resurrection as the head of the new creation.

Anointing follows redemption. The anointing comes by way of the dove, the Spirit, which is the continuation of the Lamb. The Lamb has removed sin and terminated the old creation, and the dove, the Spirit, has come to regenerate, impart life, transform, unite, and build. The dove, the Spirit, regenerates the created man, transforms the natural man, and unites the transformed man.... We may be a created man who needs to be regenerated. We may be a regenerated man who is still quite natural and who needs to be transformed. We may be a transformed man who is still separate and individualistic and who needs to be united with others. If we are properly transformed, we would be willing to be united with others. So, firstly, we need to be regenerated; secondly, we need to be transformed; and thirdly, we need to be united for the building. The dove, the Spirit, regenerates, transforms, and unites. We are all under the anointing of the dove, the Spirit. Although we may not realize it...the Lord is working to transform us.

After creation, incarnation, redemption, and anointing, we have building. This building is for the house of God. God is building a dwelling place for Himself, and He is using transformed people as the stones (John 1:42). Praise the Lord that we are not only undergoing the work of transformation, but are also in the process of building. What God needs is not a great number of stones, but a house. For eternity God needs a builded house, a Bethel, as His habitation. (*Life-study of John,* pp. 60-64)

Further Reading: Life-study of John, msg. 5

Enlightenment and inspiration: _____

_____

_____

_____

Morning Nourishment

John   ...Behold, the Lamb of God, who takes away the sin
1:29   of the world!
Acts   This man, delivered up by the determined counsel
2:23   and foreknowledge of God, you, through the hand
        of lawless men, nailed to *a cross* and killed.

The Word of God, the first crystal in the Gospel of John, refers
to Christ, the only begotten Son of God [John 1:1, 18], as the definition, explanation, and expression of God....John unveils Christ
as the great "I Am," self-existing and ever-existing (Exo. 3:14-15;
John 8:24, 28, 58). Everything other than Christ is vanity of vanities. Only He is the reality, the I Am, the One who is....Christ is
the One who is eternal, without beginning or ending (Heb. 7:3).
(*Crystallization-study of the Gospel of John*, pp. 11-12)

Today's Reading

The main stress of [John 1] is that Christ is the Word of God—
the definition, explanation, and expression of the mysterious and
invisible God. It refers to Christ in the five greatest events in the
history of the universe....John 1 reveals Christ in the creation of
all things in the beginning of time (v. 3)....Christ is also seen in the
incarnation of the invisible God to be a visible man (1:14), partaking of man's flesh and blood (Heb. 2:14), for the redemption of the
lost universe to bring in the New Testament age. The incarnated
God has blood. Acts 20:28 says that God purchased the church
with His own blood. God partook of man's flesh and blood for the
redemption of the lost universe. The entire universe, including
the heavens, was contaminated by Satan, an archangel created
by God, in his rebellion against God. This first rebel caused the
entire universe to become lost, so all things on earth and in the heavens needed to be redeemed by God (Col. 1:20)....Christ redeemed
the universe by becoming a man. The New Testament age began
at the incarnation of Christ. It is significant that the entire world
today uses one calendar, which counts the years from Christ's
incarnation. Creation brought in a universe, but this universe
became lost. Then God came to be a man by the name of Jesus

with a human nature to redeem the lost universe back to a new age, the New Testament age, starting from the day Christ was born....Christ is also revealed in His becoming the Lamb to take away the sin of the world (mankind) judicially for the New Testament (John 1:29, 36). This is the third great event in the history of the universe. When He was put to death on the cross, God considered Him the Lamb of God, who takes away the sin of the world. He became a man for the purpose of redeeming the lost universe, yet He still needed to take a further step to go to the cross to die, bearing the sins of mankind on the cross as the Lamb. (*Crystallization-study of the Gospel of John,* pp. 12-13)

[The] counsel [spoken of in Acts 2:23] must have been determined in a council held by the Divine Trinity before the foundation of the world (1 Pet. 1:20; Rev. 13:8), indicating that the Lord's crucifixion was not an accident in human history but a purposeful fulfillment of the divine counsel determined by the Triune God. (Acts 2:23, footnote 1)

Christ was foreordained, prepared, by God to be the redeeming Lamb (John 1:29) for His elect according to His foreknowledge before the foundation of the world. This was done according to God's eternal purpose and plan; it did not happen accidentally. Hence, in the eternal view of God, from the foundation of the world, that is, from the fall of man as part of the world, Christ was slain (Rev. 13:8). (1 Pet. 1:20, footnote 1)

The fourth great event in the history of the universe...is [Christ's] becoming the Spirit. John 1:32 says, "And John testified, saying, I beheld the Spirit descending as a dove out of heaven, and He abode upon Him." This is the Spirit descending as a dove upon the Lamb. Christ was the Lamb. Then He became the dove, the Spirit. Christ is revealed in John 1 in His becoming the Spirit for the transformation of God's redeemed people into stones (vv. 32-42) for the building of God's house (Bethel—v. 51) organically. (*Crystallization-study of the Gospel of John,* p. 13)

Further Reading: Crystallization-study of the Gospel of John, msg. 1

Enlightenment and inspiration: _____

_____

_____

Morning Nourishment

John **...Jesus said, You are Simon, the son of John; you**
1:42 **shall be called Cephas (which is interpreted, Peter).**
51 **...You shall see heaven opened and the angels of**
God ascending and descending on the Son of Man.

We need to be not only redeemed but also transformed. If we
were merely redeemed, we would still remain men. In order to
become like God, we need transformation. The first step of transformation is to regenerate, to remake, us. Even though we were
made in the image of God and after the likeness of God, we still do
not have anything real of God in us until we are regenerated. We
need to be regenerated to begin our transformation into stones for
God's spiritual building, His house. The house of God, Bethel, first
is the church, then the Body of Christ, and consummately the New
Jerusalem. (*Crystallization-study of the Gospel of John*, pp. 13-14)

In Matthew 16:18 the Lord mentioned this word [*Peter*, meaning
"a stone,"] when He spoke...about the building of the church. It must
have been from this that Peter obtained the concept of living stones
for the building of a spiritual house (1 Pet. 2:5), which is the church.
The stone here denotes a work of transformation that brings forth
material for God's building (1 Cor. 3:12). (John 1:42, footnote 1)

Today's Reading

John 1:51 is the fulfillment of Jacob's dream (Gen. 28:11-22).
Christ as the Son of Man, with His humanity, is the ladder set up
on the earth and leading to heaven, keeping heaven open to
earth and joining earth to heaven for the house of God, Bethel.
Jacob poured oil (a symbol of the Holy Spirit, the ultimate expression of the Triune God reaching man) upon the stone (a
symbol of the transformed man) that it might be the house of
God. Here in John 1 are the Spirit (v. 32) and the stone (v. 42) for
the house of God with Christ in His humanity. Where this is,
there is an open heaven. (John 1:51, footnote 2)

[In John 1:51] Christ is referred to in His being the heavenly
ladder to bring heaven to earth and join earth to heaven at Bethel,

the house of God, from His coming back to eternity (John 1:51; Gen. 28:11-22). We can remember these five great historical events with five words: *creation, incarnation, Lamb, Spirit,* and *ladder.* John 1 begins with Christ as the Word and ends with Him as the ladder....In order to have a ladder, there is the need of a base, and the base for Christ to be the heavenly ladder is the house of God, Bethel. The reality of Bethel is the church and then the Body of Christ and the New Jerusalem....In all these five universal, historical events, Christ, the Word of God (as: 1. the Creator in creation; 2. the man in incarnation; 3. the Lamb in redemption; 4. the Spirit in transformation; 5. the ladder in joining earth to heaven), defines, explains, and expresses the invisible God.

In His creation "the heavens are telling of the glory of God; and their expanse [firmament] is declaring the work of His hands. Day to day pours forth speech, and night to night reveals knowledge. There is no speech, nor are there words; their voice is not heard" (Psa. 19:1-3, NASB), and the invisible things of God, "both His eternal power and divine characteristics, have been clearly seen since the creation of the world" (Rom. 1:20). What is referred to in Acts 14:15-17 and 17:24-29 serves the same purpose of revealing Christ's creation speaking for God.

In His incarnation Christ unveils that the Creator has become one of His creatures (Col. 1:15), bringing God into man, mingling divinity with humanity as one, and in His human living He expresses God in the divine attributes through His human virtues. This is the new language of the new culture in the Lord's recovery.

When Jesus was born, God was brought into man and mingled Himself with man. About two thousand years ago, there was a man who was the mingling of divinity and humanity. To be a Christian means to be a man of Christ. Christ is the mingling of divinity with humanity, and we, the men of Christ, are the same. We are also the mingling of divinity with humanity. (*Crystallization-study of the Gospel of John,* pp. 14-15)

Further Reading: Crystallization-study of the Gospel of John, msg. 1

Enlightenment and inspiration: _____

_____

_____

_____

Morning Nourishment

John And John testified, saying, I beheld the Spirit descend-
1:32 ing as a dove out of heaven, and He abode upon Him.
1 Cor. So also it is written, "The first man, Adam, became a
15:45 living soul"; the last Adam *became* a life-giving Spirit.

Based on the Scriptures, the religious people were looking for a
great leader (John 1:19-25) such as Messiah, Elijah, or the Prophet
(Dan. 9:26; Mal. 4:5; Deut. 18:15, 18). But Jesus was introduced to
them as a little lamb with a little dove (John 1:29-33). The Lamb
takes sin away from man, and the dove brings God as life to man.
The Lamb is for redemption, to redeem fallen man back to God,
and the dove is for life-giving, for anointing, to anoint man with
what God is, to bring God into man and man into God, and for
uniting the believers in God. Both the Lamb and the dove are
needed for man to participate in God. (John 1:29, footnote 1)

In His becoming the Lamb for the redemption of the lost
world, Christ speaks to us how God accomplished His redemption
judicially through His death as the procedure according to His
righteousness....In His becoming the Spirit for life-giving and
transforming (1 Cor. 15:45), Christ speaks to us further how God
carries out His economy organically by His divine life for His
divine purpose according to His heart's desire. (*Crystallization-
study of the Gospel of John,* p. 15)

Today's Reading

Christ, in His being the heavenly ladder at Bethel, also speaks
to us how God desires to have a house on the earth constituted
with His redeemed and transformed elect, that He may bring
heaven to earth and join earth to heaven, to make the two as one
for eternity....The Word of God is Christ in His creation, in His
incarnation, in His becoming the Lamb, in His becoming the life-
giving Spirit, and in His being the ladder. In these five greatest
historical events, Christ speaks for God. In this sense, we may say
that the creation is the Word, the incarnation is the Word, the
Lamb is the Word, the Spirit is the Word, and the ladder is
the Word....In addition to all the above items, John, in his last

writing, Revelation, tells us that even in the warfare for the kingdom of God, Christ is the Word of God speaking for God's purpose (Rev. 19:13). When He comes to fight God's enemies for the kingdom, His name is called the Word of God. In His fighting He is God's speaking. Christ is the Word of God speaking for God's purpose. (*Crystallization-study of the Gospel of John,* pp. 15-16)

The Lord's coming back needs a solid building of His seekers. This building will be a stepping stone, a beachhead, for Him to take the earth, and it will be a mutual abode for both God and man. It will be the mingling of divinity with humanity and of humanity with divinity forever. Christ once was only divine. In order for Him to be the Son of Man, He must have the human life and the human nature. We are human, but we can be born of God to become the children of God (John 1:12-13). In order for us to be the children of God, we must have the divine life and the divine nature. Eventually, He, the divine One, will have the human life and the human nature, and we, the human ones, will have the divine life and the divine nature. Thus, He and we, we and He, will be exactly the same. This is the mingling of divinity with humanity, and this is the mutual abode of God's building. This building will be the ultimate fulfillment not only of Jacob's dream, but of God's eternal plan. It will terminate the bridge of time and usher in the blessed eternity in the future. We must be for that building and we must be that building!

After all of these five items have transpired, we shall enter into eternity future with the Lord. At that time, He will be both the Son of God and the Son of Man. As the Son of God, He will be life to us, and as the Son of Man, He will be the dwelling place for God. We shall be joined to and even mingled with Him, and we shall enjoy eternity with Him forever. Nathanael, and all of us with him, will see heaven opened and the angels of God ascending and descending on the Son of Man. This is the revelation found in John chapter one. (*Life-study of John,* p. 65)

Further Reading: Crystallization-study of the Gospel of John, msg. 1

Enlightenment and inspiration: _____

_____

_____

_____

Hymns, #187

1   O Lord, how rich Thou art to us,
    Thy love reveals the measure!
    The boundless riches of Thyself,
    In spirit here we treasure.

2   Thou art the Word, e'en God Himself,
    With God in the beginning;
    Incarnate in the flesh with us,
    And God to us defining.

3   Thou art the tabernacle true,
    In Thee we see God's glory;
    For God Thou art the temple too,
    In Thee is God's full story.

6   Thou art the Christ, the Lord of all,
    By God Thou art anointed;
    The One who is the All in all,
    For God and us appointed.

14 Thou art the spotless Lamb of God,
    Who died for our redemption;
    Thou art the Spirit-giver too,
    For our regeneration.

25 Thou art the ladder Jacob saw,
    By Thee the heav'n is open;
    In Thee we are the house of God,
    And earth is joined to heaven.

26 O Lord, Thou art the great "I AM,"
    Who all our need doth furnish;
    Enjoying Thee as all in all,
    God's purpose we accomplish.

Composition for prophecy with main point and sub-points: _____

_____
_____
_____
_____
_____
_____
_____
_____
_____
_____
_____
_____
_____
_____
_____
_____
_____
_____
_____
_____
_____
_____
_____
_____
_____
_____
_____
_____
_____
_____
_____
_____

The Building of the House of Jehovah

Scripture Reading: Hag. 1:2-5, 7-8, 9b, 14; 2:6-7, 9a

Day 1 I. The central thought of Haggai's prophecy is that
the building of the house of Jehovah is related
to the welfare of God's people today and to
the coming of the millennial kingdom with its
Messiah in the age of restoration (1:2, 8; 2:6-9,
20-23; Matt. 19:28; Acts 3:20-21):

A. In the Old Testament the house of Jehovah, or the
temple, was first a type of Christ as the house of
God individually and then a type of the church,
the Body, the enlarged Christ, as God's house corporately (John 2:19-21; 1 Tim. 3:15).

B. Because the house of Jehovah is a type of the church,
Haggai's prophecy refers to us, the New Testament
believers, since we are the reality of the type.

II. We need to see the significance of the church
as the house of Jehovah, the Father's house
(Hag. 1:2; John 14:2):

A. The church as the house of Jehovah, the Father's
house, His household, enables God's life to be prop-
agated; therefore, God's house is a place for the
continuation and multiplication of His life (vv. 2-3;
1:12-13; 20:17).

B. In the church as the house of Jehovah, the Father's
house, the invisible and mysterious Triune God
has a visible and solid manifestation among men
on earth (1 Tim. 3:15-16).

C. The church as the house of Jehovah, the Father's
house, is the dwelling place of God—the place
where God can have His satisfaction and rest; in
this dwelling place God lives and moves to accomplish His will and satisfy the desire of His heart
(Eph. 2:22; 1:5, 9, 11; Phil. 2:13).

D. As the issue of Christ's being glorified by the Father
with the divine glory, the church as the house

of Jehovah, the Father's house, is a divine and human incorporation of the processed and consummated Triune God constituted with His redeemed, regenerated, and transformed elect (John 12:23; 13:31-32; 14:2).

E. The church as the house of Jehovah, the Father's house, is for the eternal and purposeful Triune God to carry out His eternal economy to consummate the New Jerusalem as His eternal goal for His eternal expression (Eph. 3:9-11; Rev. 21:2, 10-11).

F. The church as the house of Jehovah, the Father's house, exists in the resurrection life of Christ; thus, the church is "resurrectionly"; that is, it is an organic entity absolutely in resurrection (John 11:25; 2:19; Acts 2:24).

Day 2

G. In the church as the house of Jehovah, the Father's house, we enter into the corporate experience of God and experience the All-sufficient God, who is revealed in His house (Gen. 35:1, 3, 7, 11).

III. **The New Testament reveals the way that the church as the house of Jehovah, the Father's house, is built up (Hag. 1:8, 14):**

A. The house of Jehovah, the Father's house, is built up by the mingling of divinity with humanity (John 14:20; 15:4a; 1 John 4:15):

1. The principle of God's building is that God builds Himself in Christ into us and builds us in Christ into Himself (Eph. 3:17a; John 14:20).

2. The church is God's building, composed of God Himself as the divine material mingled with man as the human material (1 Kings 6:7, 15, 20-21; 1 Cor. 3:9, 11-12a):

   a. The two natures of Christ, divinity and humanity, are joined together and mingled together as one (Luke 1:35).

   b. In principle, the church is the same as Christ—the divine nature mingled with the human nature to become one entity (John 14:20).

Day 3

B. The building up of the church as the house of Jehovah, the Father's house, is by the believers' growth in life; the growth in life is the building (1 Cor. 3:6-9, 16-17; Eph. 2:21; 4:15-16):

   1. Since God's building is living, it is growing; the actual building up of the house of God is by our growth in life, and the more we grow in life, the more we are in the building (1 Pet. 2:5; Eph. 2:21).

   2. To grow in life is to grow into the Head, Christ, and to have Christ increase in us in all things until we attain to a full-grown man (4:15, 13).

   3. The Body builds itself up by growing; growth equals building (v. 16).

C. The building up of the church as the house of Jehovah, the Father's house, is the issue of Christ making His home in our hearts (3:17a):

   1. In order for the Lord's word in Matthew 16:18 concerning the building up of the church to be fulfilled, we must allow Christ to make His home in our hearts, possessing, occupying, and saturating our inner being; this is the way to build up the church as the house of Jehovah, the Father's house.

   2. The more Christ occupies our inner being, the more we will be able to be built up with others to become the corporate expression of the Triune God (Eph. 3:17-21).

Day 4

D. The building up of the church as the house of Jehovah, the Father's house, is by the constant visitation to the redeemed elect of the Father and the Son with the Spirit who indwells the redeemed elect to be the mutual dwelling place of the consummated Triune God and His redeemed people (John 14:23; 15:4a):

   1. The Father and the Son come to visit us to do a building work in us, making an abode that will be a mutual dwelling place for the Triune God and for us (14:2, 23).

2. This is the building up of the Father's house
through the constant visitation of the Triune God.
E. The church as the house of Jehovah, the Father's
house, is built up through the practice of the scriptural way to meet and to serve (Eph. 4:11-16; 1 Cor.
14:24-26, 31; Hag. 1:8, 14):
1. The scriptural way to meet and to serve is for the
annulling of the clergy-laity system and the developing of the gifts, functions, and capacity of
all the members of the organic Body of Christ
(Matt. 20:25-28; Rom. 12:4-6).
2. Through the practice of the scriptural way to
meet and to serve, the Lord is recovering the
priesthood of the gospel (15:16), the perfecting
of the common members of the Body of Christ
to make them living, active, functioning members of the Body (Eph. 4:12, 16; Heb. 10:24-25),
and the church meetings in mutuality with
prophesying for the building up of the Body of
Christ (1 Cor. 14:4b, 24a, 26, 31).

Day 5 IV. **"I will shake all the nations, and the Desire of
all the nations will come" (Hag. 2:7a):**
A. This refers to Christ, who is the Desire of all the
nations (Mal. 3:1b).
B. The coming of Christ as the Desire of all the
nations depends on the return of God's people from
their captivity in Babylon and the recovery of the
building of God's house (1 Tim. 3:15; 1 Pet. 2:5).
C. Only the church built up as the house of God and the
Body of Christ according to the Lord's desire can be
the steppingstone into the age of the kingdom; thus,
for the sake of His coming back, the Lord needs the
church to be built up (Matt. 16:18-19, 27-28).

Day 6 V. **"I will fill this house with glory...The latter
glory of this house will be greater than the
former" (Hag. 2:7b, 9a):**
A. The glory of God is in the building of God, the house
of Jehovah (Exo. 40:34-35; 1 Kings 8:10-11; 2 Chron.
3:1; 5:1-2, 13-14; Eph. 3:21; Rev. 21:10-11).

B. In a vision of God, Ezekiel saw the glory of Jehovah return to the house of Jehovah and fill the house (Ezek. 43:1-5):
   1. The glory of Jehovah returned to the house because the building of the house was completed (vv. 2, 5).
   2. This indicates that in order for the God of glory to dwell in the church, the church must be built up to become the dwelling place of God (Eph. 2:21-22; 3:14-21).

C. In the church life the first consideration that we should have is the Lord's glory; the decisions in the church life must be made primarily according to the Lord's glory (1 Cor. 10:31; Eph. 3:21; Phil. 4:20; 1 Pet. 4:11).

D. In our experience of the church life, we need to advance so that we may experience the glory in God's dwelling place (John 17:22; Eph. 3:21).

Morning Nourishment

Hag. ...This people says, The time has not come, the
1:2 time for the house of Jehovah to be built.
   8 Go up to the mountain and bring wood and build
   the house, and I will take pleasure in it and will be
   glorified, says Jehovah.

The subject of the prophecy of Haggai is Jehovah's dealing
with the returned captives for the building of His house....
The central thought of the book of Haggai is that the building
of the house of Jehovah is related to the welfare of God's people
today and to the coming of the millennial kingdom with its Messiah in the age of restoration. In the Old Testament the house of
God, or the temple, was a type first of Christ as the house of God
individually, and then of the church, the Body, the enlarged
Christ, as God's house corporately. Thus, we should consider that
Haggai refers to us, since we are the reality of the type. Jehovah's
dealing with the returned captives signifies His dealing with us
in the recovery. (*Life-study of Haggai*, p. 2)

Today's Reading

God delights in the continuation of His life. The reason that God
has a family is because He wants to have children. Although some
families do not have children for biological reasons, in fact and in
principle, a family is called a family because it is a place where children are produced....Children are the multiplication and continuation of life. Hence, to God the first significance of a family is to
enable God's life to be multiplied and continued. This is the sym-
bolic meaning of a family, showing that God's house is a place for
the continuation and multiplication of life. This is the only place
in the universe where life can be multiplied and continued. This is
the first significance of a house. When we touch God's house, we
touch the matter of God's life, because a family is where life is continued. (*How to Administrate the Church*, pp. 10-11)

The purpose of the Father's house is first for the invisible and mysterious Triune God to have a visible and solid manifestation—the church—among men on the earth (1 Tim. 3:15-16),…to have a visible and solid household constituted by the children of God, the species of God, with His divine life for their growth in life and for His rest, satisfaction, and manifestation (Eph. 2:19). (*The Issue of Christ Being Glorified by the Father with the Divine Glory,* pp. 35, 49)

As the house of God, the church is the dwelling place of God. Ephesians 2:22 says, "In whom you also are being built together into a dwelling place of God in spirit.".…The church, the dwelling place of God on earth, is the place in which God can have His rest and put His trust. In this dwelling place God lives and moves to accomplish His will and satisfy the desire of His heart. (*The Conclusion of the New Testament,* p. 2229)

The purpose of the Father's house is also for the eternal and purposeful Triune God to carry out His eternal economy to consummate the New Jerusalem as His eternal goal for His eternal expansion and expression. The house of God, which is God's dwelling place, eventually will be the New Jerusalem, God's eternal goal for His eternal expansion and expression. (*The Issue of Christ Being Glorified by the Father with the Divine Glory,* p. 35)

The church is a new creation created in Christ's resurrection and by the resurrected Christ.…In addition to seeing [the vision] that the church was produced in Christ's resurrection, we must also see where the church is. The church today is in Christ in ascension. Ephesians 2:6 tells us that the church has been resurrected with Christ, and now the church is seated in the heavenlies with Christ. Therefore, the church is absolutely and purely of the element of Christ, absolutely in resurrection, and absolutely remaining in the heavenlies with Christ.…We must…invent some new vocabulary words to communicate such a vision of the church. We may say that today the church is "Christly," "resurrectionly," and heavenly. (*Elders' Training, Book 2: The Vision of the Lord's Recovery,* p. 38)

Further Reading: The Conclusion of the New Testament, msg. 208; *How to Administrate the Church,* ch. 1

Enlightenment and inspiration: _____

_____

_____

Morning Nourishment

John In that day you will know that I am in My Father,
14:20 and you in Me, and I in you.
1 John Whoever confesses that Jesus is the Son of God,
4:15 God abides in him and he in God.

The all-sufficient God is for the building of Bethel. God is all-sufficient for the church life, for the building of His house on earth. You cannot experience the all-sufficient God in an individualistic way. In order to experience the all-sufficient God, you must be in Bethel, in the house of God, in the church life.

God is too all-sufficient to be experienced by just a few individual believers. As individuals, we are too limited. God's all-sufficiency requires a corporate body. We need the house in order to experience this aspect of Him. (*Life-study of Genesis,* p. 1040)

Today's Reading

The church is built upon the mingling of God with man and man with God....The extent to which we are the church in reality depends upon how much this mingling has been built up in us. We may understand doctrinally that the church is a corporate entity, not individual entities, and that serving the Lord should be a Body matter, not an individual matter. However, in reality, we may still not live in the light of the church or in the mingling of God and man.

When we by the Lord's mercy allow the mingling of God with man and man with God to work and build in us, we will have the reality of the church. With resoluteness we should receive, consider, concentrate, desire, and turn our whole being toward the mingling of God and man within us. Then we will have more than a doctrinal understanding or seeing, and within us will be a genuine building work.

In order for God to enter into man, incarnation is required. In order for man to enter into God, the process of death and resurrection is required. This is the principle of God's building.

God's building work in us is the work of death and resurrection. The principle of the building of God is death and

tear down
build up

resurrection. He first tears down, and then He builds up. His tearing down is death, and His building up is resurrection. Whatever has passed through His tearing down and building up has died and resurrected. Death and resurrection bring man into God. God is in man through incarnation; man is in God through death and resurrection.

In His redemption God does not nullify our being; instead, He brings us into Himself and builds us into Himself. God is doing a work of breaking and tearing down within us for the purpose of building Himself into us and building us into Himself, to the extent that our proposals and speaking can be His proposals and speaking. (*The Church as the Body of Christ,* pp. 41, 94, 126-127)

Luke 1:35 seems to indicate that the Holy Spirit would be upon Mary only as the power for her to conceive the holy child. However, Matthew 1:18 and 20 tell us that Mary "was found to be with child of the Holy Spirit" and that "that which has been begotten in her is of the Holy Spirit." This indicates that the divine essence out of the Holy Spirit had been begotten in Mary's womb before she delivered the child Jesus. Such a conception of the Holy Spirit in the human virgin, accomplished with the divine and human essences, constituted a mingling of the divine nature with the human nature, which produced a God-man, One who is both the complete God and the perfect man, possessing the divine nature and the human nature distinctly, without a third nature being produced. (*The Conclusion of the New Testament,* pp. 2841-2842)

The principle of the Lord being a building is that God mingles Himself with humanity, and this is the principle of God's building in general. Therefore, the church also is the divine mingling of God Himself with humanity. The church is not something of the old creation. It is God's building composed of God Himself as the divine material mingled with man as the human material. In this sense, the church is a hybrid. A hybrid is a mingling of two lives and natures into one entity. (*The Building of God,* pp. 10-11)

Further Reading: The Church as the Body of Christ, chs. 3, 8, 10

Enlightenment and inspiration: _____
hybrid
_____
_____

Morning Nourishment

Eph. But holding to truth in love, we may grow up into
4:15-16 Him in all things, who is the Head, Christ, out from
whom all the Body, being joined together and
being knit together through every joint of the rich
supply and *through* the operation in the measure
of each one part, causes the growth of the Body
unto the building up of itself in love.

As believers in Christ, we need to grow and be transformed
for the building up of God's spiritual house. God's goal in the
believers is to have a house built up with spiritual stones, not
separated and scattered stones, not even a pile of stones merely
gathered together, but stones built up with one another....Grow-
ing is for building up. Although the nourishing milk of the word
is for the soul through the mind, it eventually nourishes our
spirit, making us not soulish but spiritual, suitable for building
up a spiritual house for God....The actual building of the church
as the house of God is by the growth in life of the believers. (*The
Conclusion of the New Testament*, pp. 2230-2231)

Today's Reading

To arrive at the measure of the stature of the fullness of Christ
is to arrive at the full building up of the Body of Christ. It is to
arrive at the full completion of the building up of the Body.

In Ephesians 4:14 and 15 Paul says, "That we may be no longer
little children tossed by waves and carried about by every wind of
teaching in the sleight of men, in craftiness with a view to a system
of error, but holding to truth in love, we may grow up into Him in all
things, who is the Head, Christ." "Little children" refers to those believers who are young in Christ, lacking maturity in life (1 Cor. 3:1).
To be no longer little children we need to grow up into Christ. This
is to have Christ increase in us in all things until we attain to a full-
grown man.

The word "Head" in Ephesians 4:15 indicates that our growth
in life with Christ should be the growth of the members in the Body
under the Head. This means that our growth must be in the Body.

In order to grow into the Head, we must surely be in the Body. (*The Conclusion of the New Testament,* p. 2492)

The building of the church as the Body of Christ is organic, by the growth in life. The Body of Christ is like our physical body. It is built up by its growth. Ephesians 4:15 says, "But holding to truth in love, we may grow up into Him in all things, who is the Head, Christ." Then verse 16 says, "Out from whom all the Body, being joined together and being knit together through every joint of the rich supply and through the operation in the measure of each one part, causes the growth of the Body unto the building up of itself in love." First, we must grow up into the Head in all things. Then from the Head something will come out to cause the growth of the Body. By this growth of the Body, the Body builds itself up in love. Growth equals building. The Body builds itself up by growing. This growth of the Body is not for any particular member. The Body grows for the entire Body. (*The Organic Union in God's Relationship with Man,* p. 65)

The genuine church life is the issue of Christ personally making His home in our heart to occupy every corner of our inner being. The content of the church is the Christ whom we take as our person, the Christ who is wrought into our being. In order for Christ's word in Matthew 16:18 concerning the building up of the church to be fulfilled, the church must enter into a state where many saints allow Christ to make His home in their heart, possessing, occupying, and saturating their entire inner being. The more Christ occupies our inner being, the more we will be able to be built up with others in the Body (Eph. 2:21-22; 4:16). The reality of the Body life is such an inner experience of the indwelling Christ. The Body of Christ is the consummation of our enjoyment of the unsearchable riches of Christ and the consummation of the experience of the unlimited Christ making His home in our entire inward being. The New Jerusalem is the ultimate issue of Christ making His home in our heart. (*The Conclusion of the New Testament,* p. 3391)

Further Reading: The Conclusion of the New Testament, msgs. 234, 338; *The Organic Union in God's Relationship with Man,* ch. 5

Enlightenment and inspiration: _____

_____

_____

_____

Morning Nourishment

John ...If anyone loves Me, he will keep My word, and
14:23 My Father will love him, and We will come to him
and make an abode with him.
1 Cor. What then, brothers? Whenever you come together,
14:26 each one has a psalm, has a teaching, has a revelation, has a tongue, has an interpretation. Let all
things be done for building up.

The Father's house is built up by the constant visitation
to the redeemed elect of the Father and the Son with the Spirit
who indwells the redeemed elect to be the mutual dwelling place
of the consummated Triune God and His redeemed elect....John
14:2 tells us that in the Father's house there are many abodes,
and in verse 23 we see that these abodes are built up by the
Father and the Son's visitation to those who love Him. The Spirit
is not explicitly mentioned in verse 23 but rather is implied,
for the Spirit dwells in the regenerated spirit of all those who
love the Lord Jesus. (*The Issue of Christ Being Glorified by the
Father with the Divine Glory*, p. 33)

Today's Reading

To practice the biblical way is not merely to change a way. It is to
fulfill the Lord's heart's desire according to His word concerning
the building up of His Body (Matt. 16:18; Eph. 4:12-16). This is not
merely to fulfill some of the prophecies in the New Testament. It is
to accomplish the unique, central thing in the entire universe—the
building up of the Body of Christ. (*The Scriptural Way to Meet and
to Serve for the Building Up of the Body of Christ*, p. 282)

The Lord's recovery is the recovery of the function of all the
members of the Body of Christ. The Lord desires that every member of His Body be a functioning member. Almost all Christian
groups practice the system of the clergy and laity. The clergy are
the professional preachers, pastors, and ministers, who serve God
in place of the other members of the church. Actually, the clergy
replaces the members of the Body of Christ, and this replacement
spontaneously annuls and kills the function, the capacity, and the

usefulness of the members of Christ. This is an offense to the Lord. The Lord's recovery is for the annulling of the clergy and laity and the developing of the gifts, functions, and capacity of all the members of the organic Body of Christ (Eph. 4:11-16).

The God-ordained way is to practice God's New Testament priesthood of His gospel (Rom. 15:16; 1 Pet. 2:5, 9). This way mainly consists of four practices. First, we must preach the gospel regularly by visiting sinners. God so loved the world that He gave His Son, the Savior, Christ, that the sinners, the people of the world, might believe in Him and have His eternal life (John 3:16). God desires all men to be saved (1 Tim. 2:4). The Lord's main charge to His disciples after His resurrection was to preach the gospel to all creation (Mark 16:15). To preach the gospel is the first thing the church must do for the Lord. If we mean business with the Lord in His God-ordained way, we must bear the burden to preach the gospel to get sinners saved. (*The Basic Principles for the Practice of the God-ordained Way*, pp. 2-3, 5-6)

In the present advance of the Lord's recovery, He also desires to recover the perfecting of the common members of the Body of Christ (Eph. 4:11-16). If only a small percentage of the saints in a local church are able to speak a word for the Lord and serve Him organically, this is a strong sign that this local church is short of the perfecting of the saints.

In the present advance of the Lord's recovery, He is also moving to recover the church meeting in mutuality (1 Cor. 14:23a, 26).... We have to pray, get into the Word, have our mind and spirit exercised, and have our voice exercised to share in the meetings. For the sake of the meetings, we have to exercise all the time. Our exercise will make us healthy Christians. This is for the building up organically of the church as the organic Body of Christ. (*The Present Advance of the Lord's Recovery*, pp. 13, 15-16)

Further Reading: The Issue of Christ Being Glorified by the Father with the Divine Glory, ch. 4; The Basic Principles for the Practice of the God-ordained Way

Enlightenment and inspiration: _____

_____
_____
_____

Morning Nourishment

Hag. And I will shake all the nations, and the Desire of
2:7 all the nations will come...
Matt. ...Upon this rock I will build My church, and the
16:18 gates of Hades shall not prevail against it.
27 For the Son of Man is to come in the glory of His
Father with His angels, and then He will repay
each man according to his doings.

In Haggai 2:7 we see that Christ is the Desire of all the nations. Even though the nations do not know Christ, they still desire to have Christ. All the nations desire to have peace and a good life, but the situation in the world is the opposite of this. Christ is peace; Christ is also the good life. For the nations to desire these things means that they actually desire Christ. He is the Desire of all the nations. (*Life-study of Hosea*, p. 5)

Today's Reading

Haggai 2:1-23 is the prophecy concerning the house of Jehovah in the millennium and the promise of Messiah in the coming kingdom....In verses 1 through 9 the prophet Haggai was charged to speak to the people concerning the house of Jehovah....[The] prophecy [in verses 7 through 9] concerning the house of Jehovah in the millennium was an encouragement to the building of Jehovah's house at Zerubbabel's time.

Verse 7 reveals that Christ is the Desire of all the nations. I appreciate the line in Charles Wesley's hymn that says, "Come, Desire of nations, come!" [*Hymns*, #84]. Christ truly is the desire of all mankind. All people desire to have life, light, peace, goodness, and righteousness, yet they do not realize that what they desire is really Christ. Christ is life, light, and peace. If we do not have Him, we do not have life, light, peace, or any of the human virtues. Christ is the reality of every human virtue. Thus, to desire virtue actually is to desire Christ.

According to God's arrangement in His creation of man, the human virtues, such as love, kindness, patience, and humility, are for the expression of the divine attributes. It is God's intention that the attributes of His being would be expressed by man in his virtues. As an illustration of this, consider a glove that is designed in the form of a human hand. The hand is the content of the glove, and the glove is the expression of the hand. Likewise, the human virtues are the "glove" for the expression of the divine attributes as the "hand." Just as a glove without a hand has no content, so the human virtues without the divine attributes have no reality.

Today people everywhere desire life, light, love, patience, and endurance without realizing that to desire these virtues is actually to desire Christ. All people, including unbelievers, desire Christ unconsciously. This is what it means to say that Christ is the Desire of all the nations. (*Life-study of Haggai,* pp. 5-7)

The coming of Christ as the Desire of all the nations depends on the return of God's people from their captivity in Babylon and the recovery of the building of God's house. Christ came the first time, in His incarnation, through the return of a remnant of Israel to Jerusalem from their captivity in Babylon for the rebuilding of the temple. He will come the second time through the return of a remnant of His New Testament elect from their captivity in the religious Babylon (Rev. 17) to the proper ground of the church for the recovery of the building of the church, God's spiritual house (1 Tim. 3:15; 1 Pet. 2:5). (Hag. 2:7, footnote 1)

Some say that it is impossible to have the recovery of the church life today. However, if the recovery of the church life is not possible, then the Lord Jesus has no way to come back. For the sake of His coming back, He needs the church to be built up. Only the church built up according to the Lord's desire can be the steppingstone into the age of the kingdom. In Matthew 16:18 the Lord said, "I will build My church." Therefore, we believe that it is altogether possible to have the recovery of the proper church life today. We have the Lord's promise and His word of assurance. (*Life-study of Exodus,* p. 176)

Further Reading: Life-study of Haggai, msg. 1; *Truth Lessons— Level Four,* vol. 1, lsn. 4; *Life-study of the Psalms,* msg. 11

Enlightenment and inspiration: _____

_____

_____

Morning Nourishment

Hag. 2:7 ...And I will fill this house with glory, says Jehovah of hosts.

9 The latter glory of this house will be greater than the former, says Jehovah of hosts; and in this place I will give peace, declares Jehovah of hosts.

Eph. 3:21 To Him be the glory in the church and in Christ Jesus unto all the generations forever and ever. Amen.

We are being strengthened into our inner man according to the riches of God's glory (Eph. 3:16). This glory comes to us with God and, after being worked into us, will return to God with us. By means of this two-way traffic the church, as the firstfruits in the universe (James 1:18), takes the lead to give glory to God. All the other families both in heaven and on earth will follow the church to glorify Him.

God's glory is wrought into the church, and He is expressed in the church. Hence, to God is the glory in the church; that is, God is glorified in the church. (Eph. 3:21, footnotes 1 and 2).

Today's Reading

After the completion of the building of the house, the glory of the Lord returned. In his early ministry Ezekiel had seen the glory of the Lord depart in a series of steps. First, the glory of the Lord left the temple and hesitated upon the threshold (Ezek. 9:3; 10:4). From the threshold it went out to the city. From the city the glory of the Lord went further out to the Mount of Olives on the east side of the city (11:23), and from there the glory of the Lord ascended to the heavens.

When the Lord in His leaving stopped on the threshold of the house, this indicated that He was not happy to leave. He did not want to leave, but He was forced to do so. Indicating His unwillingness to leave, He hesitated and lingered at the threshold. Eventually, He was forced to leave because of the abomination, whoredom, and degradation of the people. But now the glory of the Lord is returning by the same way He left. He departed from the east side, and now He is returning from the east (43:1-3)....It is important for us to understand why the glory of the Lord came back. The glory of the Lord returned because the building of the temple was completed. This is the crucial point. How much the Lord desires to come back to the earth! Yet, for His coming back He needs a place for the soles of His feet to rest, a place upon which He can set His feet. His habitation, His house, is the place on earth where He can put His feet.

We need to be deeply impressed with the fact that the glory of God returned only after the building of the temple was completed. If we want to dwell in the church and manifest His glory in the church, the church must be complete. If the church today corresponds to all the details of the holy building of God covered in these chapters of Ezekiel and thus is built up in every aspect, God will dwell in the church gloriously. Therefore, in order for the glorious God to dwell in the church, the church must be built up to become the dwelling place of God.

God wants to have the church built up on earth because He desires to have a dwelling place on earth....The place where He lives, His dwelling place, is the church. Since God dwells in the church, those who want to seek God and contact Him must come to the church....If we have the grace to be built up in the church, the God of glory will live among us.

In the church life we need several gates, but the most important one is the east gate—the gate that is open to the glory of the Lord. This means that in the church life we need a gate which is open to the glory of the Lord....In the church life the first consideration we should have is the Lord's glory. The decisions in the church life must be made primarily according to the Lord's glory. Even in making decisions concerning the day and time of the meetings, we should care for the Lord's glory and not simply for people's convenience. The church must be open to the Lord's glory so that His glory may come into the church. (*Life-study of Ezekiel*, pp. 273, 275-277)

Further Reading: Life-study of Ezekiel, msg. 24; *Life-study of Ephesians*, msg. 35

Enlightenment and inspiration: _____

_____

_____

Hymns, #1254

1   This is the time for building the temple of the Lord
    That all the local churches may fully be restored.
    'Tis not the time for our house while God's house
      lieth waste—
    O brothers, for God's building, rise up, make haste!

      Be strong, be strong, God's dwelling place to build!
      The Lord of hosts is with us, with His glory 'twill
        be filled!
      Be strong, be strong, and work in one accord,
      That all the nations may behold the temple of
        the Lord.

2   O hear, the Lord is speaking: Consider now your ways,
    Ye sow and bring in little, for lacking is My praise.
    Go up into the mountain, material to provide,
    And build My house that I may be glorified.

3   Ye who are priests, ye remnant of Christians now obey—
    The Lord Himself is with us, whatever men may say,
    With spirits stirred and burning, now let us come to work;
    May none his part with others in building shirk.

4   I'll fill this house with glory, the Lord of hosts has said,
    And the desire of nations will be exhibited.
    Its glory will be greater than all that's gone before,
    And we will share this glory forevermore.

Composition for prophecy with main point and sub-points: _____

_____

_____

_____

_____

_____

_____

_____

_____

_____

_____

_____

_____

_____

_____

_____

_____

_____

_____

_____

_____

_____

_____

_____

_____

_____

_____

_____

_____

_____

_____

_____

_____

_____

_____

_____

_____

_____

Experiencing the Healing Christ in Malachi
for the Lord's Second Coming
and the Consummation of the Age

Scripture Reading: Mal. 3:1-3, 10, 14; 4:2

Day 1   I. **We must see the signs of Christ's second coming and of the consummation of the age (Matt. 24:3, 14-15; Luke 21:28-36):**

A. The Lord prophesied that before Antichrist makes the covenant of seven years with the nation of Israel at the consummation of the present age, the nation of Israel would be restored (Matt. 21:19; 24:32-35; Dan. 9:27).

B. Antichrist will break his covenant with Israel, and his idol will be set up in the temple of God at the beginning of the great tribulation, which will last for three and a half years; this indicates that the temple must be rebuilt before the Lord comes back (v. 27; 2 Thes. 2:3-4).

Day 2   C. Before the great tribulation the gospel of the kingdom will be preached in the whole inhabited earth, and the overcomers will be raptured, leaving the majority of the believers, those who are not yet mature, on the earth to pass through the great tribulation (Matt. 24:14-15, 40-41; Rev. 12:5; 14:1, 4).

D. The mystery of lawlessness is working today among the nations and in human society; this lawlessness will culminate in the man of lawlessness, Antichrist (2 Thes. 2:3-10):

1. Antichrist's power will be the power of Satan; Antichrist is the embodiment of Satan; Antichrist will persecute and destroy the people of God—both the God-fearing Jews and the Christ-believing Christians (Dan. 8:24; Rev. 12:17; 13:7).

2. Antichrist will wear out the saints of the Most High; in the days before the Lord's

coming, there will be great deceit and delu-
sion, so we must persevere in and with the
Lord in this final hour (Dan. 7:25; 2 Tim. 3:1;
Mark 6:45-52).

3. Satan and Antichrist want the souls of men
to be the instruments for their activities
in the last age (Rev. 18:11-13; 2 Tim. 3:5;
cf. Zech. 12:1).

E. The mystery of godliness (Christ as the individual
manifestation of God in the flesh) is being lived out
today by the Lord's overcomers, who are the corporate manifestation of God in the flesh (1 Tim. 3:16;
Acts 9:5).

Day 3 II. **The book of Malachi reveals that as overcomers we need to experience the healing
Christ for His second coming (3:1-3; 4:2):**

A. Malachi prophesied at the time of Nehemiah; at
that time the priests and the remnant of God's
people were in the darkness of self-deception,
which is obsession (1:6-7; 1 John 1:8; Acts 9:1-2;
John 16:2; cf. Phil. 3:3):

1. The symptom of a person who is obsessed is
that what he thinks and does is totally wrong,
and yet he thinks and believes that he is
totally right.

2. Malachi shows us the degraded condition of
God's self-deceived people, who were under
Satan's authority of darkness (1:2, 6-7; 2:13-14,
17; 3:7-8, 13-15; Col. 1:12-13; cf. Acts 26:18).

Day 4 3. The children of Israel worshipped and served
God, but in their self-deception they did it
mournfully, not at all happy that they were
required to do these things (Mal. 3:13-14).

4. The reasons for obsession, self-deception, are
loving the darkness rather than the light
(John 3:19-20), pride (Obad. 3), not receiving
the love of the truth (2 Thes. 2:10-11; Prov.
23:23), and not seeking the glory that is from
the only God (John 5:44).

5. The way to be saved from obsession, self-deception, is to live in the light so that we may see what God sees (Isa. 50:10-11; Psa. 36:9; 1 John 1:5, 7, 9; Col. 1:12).

Day 5   B. The healing Christ is the Messenger of God and the living message from God as a refiner's fire and as fullers' soap to purify and refine the degraded remnant of God's people (Mal. 3:1-3; Rev. 1:20— 2:1; Amos 3:7; cf. Luke 2:26; Heb. 11:7).

C. The healing Christ is the Angel of the covenant (Mal. 3:1):

1. Christ's coming suddenly as the Angel of the covenant will be to execute upon Israel the covenant that He enacted through His death (Matt. 26:28).

2. In His first coming Christ came in the way of an Angel, a serving one (cf. Heb. 1:14), to serve God in forming the new testament (Mark 10:45).

3. When Christ established His table on the night in which He was betrayed, He established the new covenant (Luke 22:20), in which God is obligated to forgive our sins and to dispense Himself into our being to be our life, our law of life, and our everything as our inward content so that we may live Him (Jer. 31:31-34; Heb. 8:8-12).

4. As the Angel of the covenant, Christ in resurrection executes the new covenant as its surety (7:22), making it real to us by assuring us that our sins have been forgiven and by dispensing the riches of the covenanted Triune God into us.

D. The healing Christ is the Desire of the nations (Mal. 3:1; Hag. 2:7).

Day 6   E. The healing Christ is the Sun of righteousness (Mal. 4:2; 3:1-3):

1. The word *Sun* indicates life, and the word *righteousness* indicates justice; the whole earth is

filled with death and injustice, but with the healing Christ we have life and justice (cf. 2 Cor. 5:4; Heb. 6:10).

2. In His first coming Christ was the dawning Sun to the dark age; in His second coming Christ will return as the Sun of righteousness in His kingdom (Luke 1:78; Mal. 4:2; cf. Matt. 17:1-8).

3. As the Sun of righteousness with healing in His wings, Christ heals us in life (Mal. 4:2; John 1:4-5; 8:12).

4. To be healed is to be saved, to be made whole; Christ will heal us, but we must give Him the freedom to use His wings to fly above us, around us, through us, and within us (Mal. 4:2; Prov. 4:18):

a. We must see God's great love for us and keep ourselves in the love of God (Mal. 1:1-2; Eph. 1:4-5; 2 Cor. 5:14; Jude 19-21; 2 Thes. 3:5).

b. We must take heed to our spirit, exercise our spirit, not grieving or quenching the Spirit (Mal. 2:15-16; Eph. 4:30; 1 Thes. 5:19; Rom. 8:6).

c. We must honor and fear God by bringing the whole tithe into the storehouse for the need of the church, the advancement of the gospel, the supply of the Lord's servants, and the supply of the needy saints (Mal. 3:7-12; Deut. 14:22-23; Phil. 1:5; 4:15-16; 3 John 5-8; Rom. 12:13):

(1) Although the word concerning the tithe was spoken to the Israelites in the Old Testament, in principle it applies also to the New Testament believers (Mal. 3:10; cf. Heb. 7:1-3; Matt. 23:23).

(2) If we would be faithful to live for God's administration in caring for money and material matters, there would be no

financial needs in the recovery (Neh. 13:10-14; Luke 6:38; Acts 20:35; Matt. 6:1-4).

5. The overcomers, who are reconstituted with Christ as the Sun, will shine forth like the sun in the kingdom of their Father (13:43; Judg. 5:31).

Eph 4:30 "And do not grieve the Holy spirit of God..."

to displease Him.

The Holy spirit abides in us forever, never leaving us. He is grieved when we don't walk accordy to Him & when we don't live accord to the principle of reality w/ grace to the details of our daily walk.

1 Thes. 5:19 "Don't quench the spirit."

The "spirit causes our spirit to be buried.

The mind set on the flesh, it's death, the mind set on the spirit, it's life & peace.

Morning Nourishment

Matt. And as He sat on the Mount of Olives, the disciples
24:3 came to Him privately, saying, Tell us, When will
these things be? And what will be the sign of Your
coming and of the consummation of the age?
15 Therefore when you see the abomination of desolation, which was spoken of through Daniel the
prophet, standing in the holy place (let him who
reads understand).

[Antichrist] will make a covenant with Israel for seven years
and permit them to freely worship God. After three and a half
years, Antichrist will be slain temporarily; then the spirit of the
fifth Caesar (Nero) of the Roman Empire will come up out of
the abyss and enter into the dead body of Antichrist to resurrect
him to be the eighth Caesar. Antichrist will break the covenant
and begin to persecute the Israelites and the Christians. He will
also set up his image in the temple (Matt. 24:15; 2 Thes. 2:4), until
the complete destruction that is determined will be poured
out upon the desolator, that is, upon Antichrist (Dan. 9:27). (*The
Up-to-date Presentation of the God-ordained Way and the Signs
concerning the Coming of Christ*, p. 55)

Today's Reading

In Matthew 24 the Lord gave a clear revelation concerning the
restoration of Israel. In verse 32 the Lord said, "But learn the parable from the fig tree: As soon as its branch has become tender and
puts forth its leaves, you know that the summer is near." To the
saints, the fig tree is a sign of the consummation of the age....
The fig tree is a symbol of the nation of Israel (Jer. 24:2, 5, 8). Because Israel was stubborn and rebellious and had no fruit that
could satisfy God, she was rejected by God [cf. Matt. 21:19]. In A.D.
70, Titus, the Roman prince, brought with him a great army to destroy Jerusalem and the temple, as prophesied by the Lord...
(Matt. 24:2). From that time, the children of Israel were scattered
among the nations. Not only did their nation fall, but even their
homeland was lost. Humanly speaking, there was truly no hope for

the nation of Israel to be reformed. However, the Bible contains a prophecy saying that one day the cursed and dried up fig tree would become tender and put forth leaves.

Concerning the rebuilding of the temple, first we need to see the two halves of the last week. The last week will be cut into two halves by Antichrist's abolishing of the seven-year covenant he will make with Israel. In the first three and a half years, Antichrist will support the children of Israel, permitting them to freely worship God; in the latter three and a half years, Antichrist will cause the sacrifice and the oblation to cease (Dan. 12:7; 9:27) and replace them with an idol of himself. In Matthew 24:15, the holy place in which Antichrist's image will stand refers to the sanctuary within the temple (Psa. 68:35; Ezek. 7:24; 21:2) and the abomination refers to the image of Antichrist as an idol. In other words, the idol will remain in the temple for three and a half years until Christ will destroy Antichrist by the manifestation of His coming. Therefore, first the temple will have to be rebuilt; then the children of Israel will be able to worship God and offer sacrifices to Him, and Antichrist will be able to set up his image.

Before the great tribulation, the overcomers will be raptured, leaving the majority of the believers, those who are not yet mature, on the earth to pass through the great tribulation. Matthew 24:40-41...indicates that while the worldly people are befuddled by material things, with no sense of the coming judgment, some of the sober and watchful believers will be taken away. To the befuddled and senseless people, this should be a sign of Christ's coming. Therefore, we should take heed to ourselves, lest at some time our hearts be weighed down with debauchery and drunkenness and the anxieties of life (Luke 21:34), and we miss the rapture and become like Lot's wife. (*The Up-to-date Presentation of the God-ordained Way and the Signs concerning the Coming of Christ,* pp. 56-59)

Further Reading: The Up-to-date Presentation of the God-ordained Way and the Signs concerning the Coming of Christ, ch. 6

Enlightenment and inspiration: _____

_____

_____

_____

Morning Nourishment

Matt. And this gospel of the kingdom will be preached in
24:14 the whole inhabited earth for a testimony to all the
nations, and then the end will come.

Dan. And he will speak things against the Most High and
7:25 wear out the saints of the Most High...and they will
be given into his hand for a time and times and half
a time.

This gospel of the kingdom will be preached in the whole earth
for a testimony to all the nations before the end of this age. Hence,
that preaching, signified by the white horse of the first seal in Revelation 6:1-2, will be a sign of the consummation of this age....This
testimony must spread to the whole earth before the end of this
age, the time of the great tribulation. (Matt. 24:14, footnotes 1 & 2)

Today's Reading

The lawlessness that will characterize Antichrist (2 Thes. 2:3)
is already operating in this age mysteriously. It is the mystery of
lawlessness working today among the nations and in human
society. (2 Thes. 2:7, footnote 1)

Antichrist will be the last of the false Christs and will work
signs and lying wonders with the power of Satan in order to
deceive the perishing (2 Thes. 2:3, 9-10). (Matt. 24:24, footnote 1)

Mrs. Penn-Lewis once said, "Many believers say that they
have encountered a lot of pressure. The battle now seems to grow
thicker day by day. It seems as if we are the only target of Satan.
But the question now is whether you can persevere through the
final half-hour....To wear out [in Daniel 7:25] is to consume. Now
the work of consuming the saints has already begun. It is harder
to recognize Satan as the one who consumes the saints than to
recognize him as the roaring lion."

In the days before the Lord's coming, there will be great deceit
and delusion. If it has its way, even the elect will be deceived. Furthermore, the "form of godliness" will exceedingly increase. The de-
crease of faith will be due not only to the love of the world and the
denial of God's Word, but will also be due to the false faith

fashioned by Satan. One brother said, "These works of Satan will become an invisible influence in the air surrounding us. They will become a form of godliness, which will be inhabited by the evil spirits and which will be occupied with the oppression of Hades. These evil spirits will do their utmost to harm, deceitfully lead, confuse, and oppress God's children. They will affect our bodies, suppress our mood, and darken our mind. Various strange feelings and trials unheard of in the past will come upon us and will strip us in a surprising way of all willingness and ability to incline toward God. Our spirit will be tired and weak, our mind will be dull, and our will will slumber. We will be strangely covetous of the things which God forbids and will surprisingly love the amusement and customs of this world. We will find it difficult to preach with full freedom and power and will find hard to listen attentively to a message or kneel down to give ourselves to prayer continually. At such a time as today, when the evening is at hand, we must quell this kind of atmosphere!" Oh, let us be strong in the Lord! Satan will certainly endeavor with unthinkable power to deceive our mind and our will; he will make it difficult for us to carry on an intimate walk with the Lord, and we will find it easy to live according to the flesh and harder to faithfully serve God and give ourselves to prayer. It will seem as if our entire being is stirred up to oppose our following the Lord Jesus to the end and seduce us to make a covenant with the world. (*The Collected Works of Watchman Nee*, vol. 10, pp. 428-429, 431)

Through [the outpouring of the Spirit] the individual Christ became the corporate Christ (1 Cor. 12:12-13), the church as the great mystery of godliness, God manifested in the flesh (1 Tim. 3:15-16). The church as the manifestation of Christ will bring in the glorious day of restoration, the age of the millennial kingdom (Joel 3:16-21), in which Christ will be manifested in a fuller way. The restoration will consummate in the fullest manifestation of Christ in the New Jerusalem in the new heaven and new earth. (Joel 2:28, footnote 1)

Further Reading: The Collected Works of Watchman Nee, vol. 10, pp. 423-433

Enlightenment and inspiration: _____

_____

_____

Morning Nourishment

Mal. A son honors *his* father, and a servant his lord.
1:6-7 Therefore if I am a Father, where is My honor? And
if I am the Lord, where is My fear? says Jehovah of
hosts to you, O priests who despise My name. But
you say, How have we despised Your name? You
offer defiled food upon My altar. And you say, How
have we defiled You? In that you say, The table of
Jehovah is despicable.
1 John If we say that we do not have sin, we are deceiving
1:8 ourselves, and the truth is not in us.

Spiritual reality is that which is true. It is the truth that sets
us free. However, a Christian often does not touch that which is
true; instead, he falls into falsehood, and he is deceived and
bound by the deception. He does not see the true nature of matters, but is deceived to think that he is very clear. What he thinks
and does is totally wrong, and yet he thinks that he is very right.
This kind of condition is known as "obsession." Those who are
obsessed need God's light before they can be delivered from their
obsession. (*The Collected Works of Watchman Nee*, vol. 36, p. 257)

Today's Reading

Obsession is self-deception. An obsessed person is like the person described in 1 John 1:8....If a man knows that he has sinned, yet
tells others that he has not sinned, this is a lie. But if a man has
sinned, yet believes that he has not sinned, this is self-deception. Lying is knowing that one has sinned but telling others that he has not
sinned. Being obsessed is having clearly sinned yet, at the same
time, thinking that one is as wonderful and as sinless as the Lord Jesus, even to the point that he believes and says that he has no sin.
Lying is knowing that one has sinned and trying to deceive others.
Being obsessed is believing that one has no sin and telling others
that he has no sin, when he has really sinned. In other words, lying is
deceiving others, while being obsessed is deceiving oneself. The content of lying and obsession are the same; there is sin in both cases.
But in one case, a man's conscience knows that he has sinned, yet he

deceives others by saying that he has not sinned. In the other case, a man's mind tells him that he has not sinned, and in his heart he also believes that he has not sinned. Those who deceive others are lying, while those who deceive themselves are obsessed. All obsessed persons are self-deceiving persons. All obsessed persons spend so much time considering themselves that they fall into obsession. Many proud people have become obsessed because they not only try to make others believe that they are a certain kind of person, but they themselves believe that they are that kind of person!

Obsession is a matter of the heart. It is doing the wrong thing yet saying in the heart that it is right. If a man does something wrong, yet stubbornly says with his mouth that it is right, this is lying. But if a man does something wrong, and not only says with his mouth but even believes in his heart that it is right, this is obsession.

The symptom of obsession is thinking and believing that a wrong thing is right to the point that one cannot say that it is wrong. This is being obsessed. There are those who imagine that something is happening with others when nothing actually is happening. The imagination goes so far that they become convinced of a certain matter, and they even come up with proofs and evidences to support their imagination. This also is obsession. Some Christians want to do something or desire to achieve certain goals. In the beginning they have some feeling that what they want to do may not be right. But later, as their thoughts are set in that direction, the more they think about it, the more they feel that it is right, and the more real and true the things become. In the end, they believe that it is absolutely right. They consider it to be the truth, and they tell others that it is the truth. This also is obsession. One can be so obsessed that when others use God's Word and prove to him that he is wrong, he will still not take heed. It is not easy to help or correct an obsessed Christian, because he believes that his conscience says he is right. (*The Collected Works of Watchman Nee,* vol. 36, pp. 257-259)

Further Reading: The Collected Works of Watchman Nee, vol. 36, pp. 257-271

Enlightenment and inspiration: _____

_____

_____

Morning Nourishment

Mal. I have loved you, says Jehovah; but you say, How
1:2 have You loved us? Was not Esau Jacob's brother,
declares Jehovah? Yet I loved Jacob.
3:13-14 Your words have been strongly against Me, says
Jehovah; but you say, What have we spoken against
You? You say, It is vain to serve God; and what profit
is it that we have kept His charge and have walked
mournfully before Jehovah of hosts?

In Malachi 3:13 through 18 we see Jehovah's encouragement
to those who fear Him and serve Him....The words of some of
the sons of Jacob were strongly against Jehovah (v. 13a)....They
said, "It is vain to serve God"...(v. 14). They worshipped and
served God, but they did it mournfully, not at all happy that they
were required to do these things.

Those who spoke strongly against Jehovah also said, "Now
we call the arrogant blessed; not only have those who act wickedly been built up, but they also try God and escape" (v. 15). This
indicates that these opposers of God seemed to be saying, "The
way to be blessed is not to be humble but to be arrogant.
The ones who act wickedly not only are built up, but they try
God, not believing Him and not giving Him the tithe, and
they escape from any kind of calamity. Instead of suffering, they
escape tribulation." (*Life-study of Malachi,* pp. 15-16)

Today's Reading

We must be very careful not to have any intention of deceiving
others. Even when we say something inaccurate by accident, we
should correct it. If we try to consciously say an inaccurate word,
we will first deceive others, but in the end, we will fall into self-
deception.

In the Old Testament, there is one book, [Malachi,] which
shows us what obsessed people are like....In 1:2 it says, "I have
loved you, says Jehovah." This is a fact. Yet the Israelites said,
"How have You loved us?" This is obsession. The word which came
out of the mouth of the Israelites was different from ordinary

lying. They were not afraid to say to God, "How have You loved us?" This proves that they sincerely believed in their heart that God had not loved them. They did not believe the facts; they took falsehood as truth. This is being obsessed.

Malachi 1:6 says, "A son honors his father, and a servant his lord. Therefore if I am a Father, where is My honor? And if I am the Lord, where is My fear? says Jehovah of hosts to you, O priests who despise My name." This is God's word. Yet they said, "How have we despised Your name?" They did not fear Jehovah, yet they believed that they had not despised His name. This is obsession.

Malachi 2:13 says, "And this second thing you do: You cover the altar of Jehovah with tears, with weeping and sighing, so that He no longer regards the sacrifice or receives it with pleasure from your hand." These are facts. Yet they said, "For what reason?" (v. 14). They did something wrong, yet they did not believe that there was such a thing. This is obsession.

Malachi 3:7 says, "From the days of your fathers you have turned aside from My statutes and have not kept them. Return to Me, and I will return to you, says Jehovah of hosts." This is God's word. Yet they asked God, "How shall we return?" It seems as if they had never gone away from God's ordinances. They believed that they did not need to turn any further. This is obsession.

Verse 8 says, "Will a man rob God? Yet you have robbed Me." This is God's word. Yet they said, "How have we robbed You?" They robbed God, yet they believed that they had not done anything. This is obsession.

Verse 13 says, "Your words have been strongly against Me, says Jehovah." This is a fact. Yet they said, "What have we spoken against You?" Their words had been strong against God, yet they believed that they had not done anything. This is obsession. (*The Collected Works of Watchman Nee*, vol. 36, pp. 259-261)

Further Reading: Life-study of Malachi, msg. 3

Enlightenment and inspiration: _____

_____ Fact - God loved the Israel
_____ but they doubt God's words
_____ questioning - that is obsession.

Morning Nourishment

Mal. I am about to send My messenger, and he will clear
3:1-3 the way before Me; and suddenly the Lord, whom
you seek, will come to His temple. And the Angel of
the covenant, whom you desire, He will come, says
Jehovah of hosts. And who will endure the day of
His coming? And who will stand when He appears?
For He is like a refiner's fire and like fullers' soap.
And He will sit as a refiner and a purifier of silver,
and He will purify the sons of Levi and purge them
like gold and like silver, and they will offer to Jehovah a sacrifice in righteousness.

The book of Malachi reveals Christ in His first coming and in
His second coming. In His first coming He is the Messenger of
God. As the Messenger of God, Christ not only brings a word or
a message from God to God's people; He Himself is the living
message. This is fully proved by the four Gospels, which are a
complete and perfect record of Christ as the living message sent
by God to His chosen people. While the Lord Jesus was living on
earth, as He traveled through the cities and as He spoke to the
people, ministering Himself into the intrinsic part of their being,
He Himself was the message. (*Life-study of Malachi,* p. 9)

Today's Reading

Jehovah's dealing with the sons of Levi is to refine and purify
the priests by His coming as the Messenger of Jehovah (Mal.
3:1-4)....This prophecy has a threefold fulfillment.

First, this prophecy was fulfilled in the coming of the prophet
Malachi, the type of Christ as the coming One....Second, this
prophecy was fulfilled in the first coming of Christ with John the
Baptist as His forerunner (Matt. 11:7-13). In His first coming,
Christ came as a Messenger and even as the message sent by
God to adjust, refine, and purify the priests. In the Gospels the
Lord Jesus frequently rebuked the priests....Third, this proph-
ecy will be fulfilled in the second coming of Christ with Elijah as
His forerunner (Isa. 40:3-5, 9-11; Matt. 17:11; Rev. 11:3-4).

Christ will come suddenly as the Angel of the covenant, whom the people of Israel seek and whom the people of Israel desire (Mal. 3:1; Hag. 2:7a)....Christ's coming suddenly as the Angel of the covenant will be to execute upon Israel the covenant that He enacted through His death (Matt. 26:28). He came in the sense of an Angel to serve God in forming the new testament. When He established His table on the night in which He was betrayed, the Lord Jesus told us that He was enacting the new covenant: "This cup is the new covenant established in My blood" (Luke 22:20). Thus He formed the new testament, in which God is obligated to dispense Himself into our being to be our life, our life law, and our everything as our content. Although the Lord Jesus enacted the new covenant nearly two thousand years ago, generally speaking the Jewish people have not benefitted by it. Instead, the benefit has gone to the Gentiles. However, when Christ comes back, He will come as the Angel of the covenant to execute His covenant over the repentant and believing Jews. At that time they will become beneficiaries of the new covenant.

Christ will come also to refine and purify the sons of Levi, mainly the priests, like a refiner's fire and like fullers' soap that they may offer to God the proper sacrifice (Mal. 3:2-4). In the millennium the repentant Jews who are regenerated through the new covenant will be the priests to take care of all the nations. For this they will need much refining and purifying. Therefore, in His second coming Christ will renew, sanctify, and transform Israel to be His refined and purified priests.

In His second coming, Christ will be the Angel of the covenant, the Desire of nations (3:1), and the Sun of righteousness (4:2). Actually, Christ was the Angel of the covenant even in His first coming. As the Angel of the covenant, Christ enacted the new covenant. Before going to the cross, the last thing He did was to establish the new covenant at His table (Matt. 26:26-30). (*Life-study of Malachi*, pp. 5-7, 9)

Further Reading: Life-study of Malachi, msg. 1

Enlightenment and inspiration: _____

_____

_____

_____

Morning Nourishment

Mal. But unto you who fear My name will the Sun of
4:2 righteousness arise with healing in His wings, and
you will go forth and leap about like well-fed calves.
Matt. Then the righteous will shine forth like the sun in
13:43 the kingdom of their Father....

Based upon [His] new covenant (Heb. 8:10-12), we are forgiven
by God, who even forgets our failures. God is then able to dispense
Himself into our intrinsic being to be our life, to be the law of life,
and to be everything to us as our inward content that we may live
Him. This means that the new covenant is to make us absolutely
one with God. He becomes us, and we, being constituted with Him,
are one with Him in His life and nature. (*Life-study of Malachi*, p. 10)

Today's Reading

God has been constituted into us to become us and...we have
become one with God in His life and nature. The New Testament
reveals that God is our Father and that we are His sons. We are
not sons who have been adopted by God but sons who have been
born of God. God is our Father because He has begotten us, and
we are His sons because we have been born of Him. Just as a
child shares the life and nature of his father but not the fatherhood, so we as sons born of God share God's life and nature but
not His fatherhood nor His Godhead. We are the same as God
our Father in life and nature, but we surely are not God in His
Godhead or the Father in His fatherhood. This is the intrinsic
revelation of the Bible, especially of the New Testament.

In our daily living, we need to remember our status as sons of
God possessing the life and nature of God. For example, if a brother
and his wife both realize this, knowing that they are not only human but also divine, they will respect each other to the uttermost.
Instead of disputing, they will honor each other and be kind to each
other....We should not forget our status as sons of God.

In His second coming, Christ will also be the Desire of the nations (Mal. 3:1; Hag. 2:7). Christ is the One whom we desire. Day by
day we desire Him to be our love, our humility, our meekness,

and our joy. Nothing is better than joy. This joy becomes our strength, our healing, our feeding, and our nourishment. Real joy comes from Christ being our life, our virtues, and our everything. I can testify that I have been loving this One for over seventy years, and I love Him today much more than ever. Daily I desire Him, love Him, and consider Him. He surely is our Desire.

As the Sun of righteousness, Christ will come with healing in His wings (Mal. 4:2). Today the Pentecostal people practice what is called divine healing. Actually, Christ Himself is our healing. He is the Sun that heals us as it shines upon us.

In His first coming, the earth rejected Christ; therefore, the earth lacks His healing. But because we have received Him in a secret, hidden way, we receive His healing every day. His healing causes us to have joy so that we forget our anger and anxiety. We are sick from sin, death, and many deficiencies and imperfections. Only this healing Christ can make us whole. To be healed is to be saved. To be healed, to be saved, is to be made whole. He will heal us, but we must give Him the freedom to use His wings to fly above us, around us, and within us.

In His first coming, Christ healed the degraded priesthood, but in His second coming, He will heal the remnant of the people of Israel. Then He will be everything to the earth and to us. This healing Christ will come suddenly. Thus, we need to be alert, ready to receive Him.

The center of the book of Malachi is the healing Christ. This healing Christ is the Messenger of God, the Angel of the covenant, and the Desire of the nations. Christ's being our healing is based upon His being the Sun of righteousness. The word "Sun" indicates life, and the word "righteousness" indicates justice. The whole earth is filled with death and injustice, but with the healing Christ we have life and justice. We are waiting for Him to come as the Sun of righteousness with healing in His wings. (*Life-study of Malachi*, pp. 10-12)

Further Reading: Life-study of Malachi, msg. 2

Enlightenment and inspiration: _____
_____
_____
_____

Hymns, #200

1   Thou art the Sun of righteousness
        With healing in Thy wings;
    The shining of Thy glorious face
        To us Thy riches brings.

2   The tender mercy of our God
        Caused Thee on us to dawn,
    To those in darkness giving light
        That shades of death be gone.

3   Thou art the Morning without clouds,
        And as the Morning Light;
    We are the tender grass on earth,
        Who in Thy rays delight.

4   Thy shining light with pleasant rays
        Increases all the way;
    It shines within us more and more
        Until the perfect day.

5   It shines thru woe with clearest beams,
        As shining after rain;
    And in Thy mercy with Thy love
        Thy shining e'er remains.

6   Thou also art the Morning Star
        To us as a reward;
    While still 'tis dark it shines with light
        To those who love the Lord.

7   Lord, help us e'er to love Thy light
        And see things from afar;
    And look for Thee in watch and prayer
        As for the Morning Star.

Composition for prophecy with main point and sub-points: _____

The Revival Revealed in the Minor Prophets

Scripture Reading: Hab. 3:2a; Hosea 6:2; Joel 2:28-29; Hag. 1:14a; 2:7a; Mal. 3:1b; 4:2

Day 1
I. **Habakkuk 3:2a speaks of revival—"O Jehovah, revive Your work / In the midst of the years":**
   A. We may say that this matter of revival is the "kernel" within the "shell" of the books of the Minor Prophets.
   B. Among God's elect there has always been an aspiration to be revived; although we may not realize it, such an aspiration has been within us through all the years of our Christian life (cf. Psa. 80:17-19).
   C. In the eyes of God, one person among His elect represents the whole; God always considers His elect as a corporate Body.
   D. This means that Habakkuk and we are one in the unit of God's elect; thus, when Habakkuk prayed for revival, we also prayed; such a prayer is an everlasting prayer.
   E. In order to practice the God-ordained and scriptural way to meet and to serve, we need to be revived; this is why the Lord leads us to practice morning revival:
      1. We believers should follow the sunrising to be revived and to have a new beginning every morning; every day we need a "sunrising," and this sunrising is a revival (Mal. 4:2; Prov. 4:18; Judg. 5:31; Matt. 13:43).
      2. If we experience a daily revival, then we will be living and qualified to practice the God-ordained way and to help the church to take this way.

Day 2
II. **On the one hand, Habakkuk prayed for revival; on the other hand, Hosea spoke of the desolation of the "two days" and the resurrection on the third day—"He will enliven us after two days; / On the third day He will raise us up, / And we will live in His presence" (Hosea 6:2):**

A. With the Lord one day is like a thousand years (2 Pet. 3:8); according to this principle, the two days in Hosea 6:2 may signify the first two periods of a thousand years each, counting from A.D. 70, when the Roman prince Titus destroyed Jerusalem and the temple, cruelly killed thousands of Jews, and scattered the Jews among the nations.

B. From that time Israel, our representative, has been desolate; from that time the Jews have been without king, without prince, without sacrifice, and without the temple, fulfilling Hosea's prophecy in 3:4.

C. For two thousand years God has left Israel in a dead condition, but after this two-thousand-year period the third thousand years will come.

D. The third day may signify a third period of a thousand years, that is, the millennium, the age of restoration, which will be in the reality of Christ's resurrection (Rev. 20:6); at that time Israel will be raised up, that is, restored.

E. This principle is the same in our Christian life:

    1. After the two days of desolation there is the third day; Christ was resurrected on the third day, and as the pneumatic Christ, the life-giving Spirit, in resurrection, He is the reality of the third day (1 Cor. 15:4, 45; John 11:25).

    2. Today we may receive the pneumatic Christ in resurrection and thus enjoy the reality of His resurrection; if we have the resurrected Christ, we are in the morning, the sunrising, and this is a real revival to us.

    3. Whenever we contact such a Christ, we are brought from the desolation of the two days to the resurrection of the third day.

Day 3

F. The revival revealed in the Minor Prophets can be applied to the family, to the church, to the nations, to the entire human race, and even to the whole universe; in principle, everything and everyone on earth are in the desolation of the two days spoken of in Hosea 6:2:

1. Since the fall of man, there has been in all of creation an aspiration for revival; concerning this, Romans 8:20-22 says, "The creation was made subject to vanity, not of its own will, but because of Him who subjected it, in hope that the creation itself will also be freed from the slavery of corruption into the freedom of the glory of the children of God. For we know that the whole creation groans together and travails in pain together until now."

2. As a result of Adam's fall, corruption, slavery, and death have come into the whole creation; today everything is decaying and is under the slavery of corruption; all the things that are under this slavery aspire to be revived (cf. 2 Cor. 4:16).

G. The universal need for revival, for restoration, can be met only by Christ and in Christ; only Christ, who was resurrected on the third day, is the renewing power:

1. For the whole universe and for all mankind, Christ is the resurrection, the reality of the third day; the reality of the third day is the person of the resurrected Christ with the reality of revival.

2. Christ, therefore, is the element of the revival for which all creation aspires; the corruption and desolation can be swallowed up only by the resurrected Christ.

H. The way to experience revival is to contact Christ by repenting and confessing our sins, failures, and darkness, thereby entering into Him as the resurrection; by doing this, we are brought from the desolation of the two days to Christ as the reality of the third day; the third day is nothing other than the person of the resurrected Christ with the reality of revival.

Day 4   III. Joel 2:28 and 29 speak of the outpouring of the Spirit:

A. Every day we need the outpouring of the all-inclusive, consummated, compound, life-giving Spirit as the processed and consummated Triune God.

B. This Spirit includes Christ's divinity and humanity, the effectiveness of His death, and the power of His resurrection; this Spirit is our portion, our inheritance.

IV. **The response of God's elect is to be stirred up in their spirit by the Lord: "Jehovah stirred up the spirit of Zerubbabel the son of Shealtiel, the governor of Judah, and the spirit of Joshua the son of Jehozadak, the high priest, and the spirit of all the remnant of the people" (Hag. 1:14a):**

A. For the recovery of the building of God's house, God's elect were stirred up by the Lord in their spirit in the order of God's authority, beginning with Zerubbabel the governor (cf. Ezra 1:5).

B. In the Minor Prophets both the divine Spirit and the stirred-up human spirit of God's elect are mentioned.

C. In the New Testament the divine Spirit has been consummated and poured out (Acts 2:17-21; Joel 2:28-32), and our human spirit responds to such a Spirit by being stirred up (2 Tim. 1:6-7; cf. Acts 17:16; Rom. 8:16; 2 Cor. 2:13).

Day 5 V. **The Minor Prophets also reveal that Christ is our enjoyment; the enjoyment of God's Christ is actually the enjoyment of God Himself (Psa. 43:4):**

A. "I will shake all the nations, and the Desire of all the nations will come" (Hag. 2:7a; cf. Mal. 3:1b):

  1. We may enjoy Christ as the Desire of God's elect and the One desired by mankind; whether we are hot or cold toward the Lord, we desire Christ; every day we desire Christ.

  2. Even though the nations do not know Christ, they still desire Christ; all people desire to have

peace and a good life with virtues such as light, love, patience, humility, meekness, endurance, joy, and righteousness; since Christ is the reality of these things, for the nations to desire these things means that, unconsciously, they desire Christ.

3. Christ is mankind's unique need; everyone, the believers and the unbelievers alike, desires Christ.

B. We may enjoy Christ as the Angel of the covenant (v. 1b):

1. For Him to be the Angel means that He is a serving one (cf. Heb. 1:14).

2. As the Angel of the covenant, He enacted the new covenant at His table (Luke 22:20), and as its surety (Heb. 7:22), He makes everything in it a reality to us (Jer. 31:31-34; Heb. 8:8-12).

Day 6   C. Malachi 4:2 tells us that we may enjoy Christ as the Sun of righteousness with healing in His wings:

1. As the Sun of righteousness, Christ is our enjoyment for our growing in life, in the dispelling of the darkness.

2. As the Sun of righteousness, Christ is our enjoyment for our healing in life, in the effacing of unrighteousness.

VI. **When we have Christ, we not only have revival—we have restoration:**

A. The millennial kingdom will be a time of restoration (Matt. 19:28; Acts 3:21); this restoration will consummate in the new heaven and new earth with the New Jerusalem as the center.

B. That will be the ultimate, the consummate, restoration accomplished by the resurrected Christ.

VII. **The Lord desires to bring the churches into a new revival to end this age:**

A. We can enter into a new revival by arriving at the highest peak of the divine revelation through the ministry of the age—the revelation of the eternal economy of God: "I hope that the saints in all the churches throughout the earth, especially the co-workers and the elders, will see this revelation and then rise up to pray that God would give us a new revival—a revival which has never been recorded in history" (*Life-study of 1 & 2 Chronicles,* p. 15).

B. We can enter into a new revival by living the life of a God-man: "We should all declare that we want to live the life of a God-man. Eventually, the God-men will be the victors, the overcomers, the Zion within Jerusalem. This will bring in a new revival which has never been seen in history, and this will end this age" (*Life-study of 1 & 2 Chronicles,* p. 28).

C. We can enter into a new revival by shepherding people according to God: "I hope that there will be a genuine revival among us by our receiving this burden of shepherding. If all the churches receive this teaching to participate in Christ's wonderful shepherding, there will be a big revival in the recovery" (*The Vital Groups,* p. 40).

Morning Nourishment

Hab. ...O Jehovah, revive Your work in the midst of the
3:2 years; in the midst of the years make *it* known...
Psa. Let Your hand be upon the man of Your right hand,
80:17-19 upon the son of man whom You have strengthened
for Yourself;...Revive us, and we will call upon
Your name. O Jehovah God of hosts, restore us;
cause Your face to shine, and we will be saved.

In his prayer for revival, Habakkuk represents all God's elect throughout the generations [Hab. 3:2]. Among God's elect there has always been an aspiration to be revived. Moreover, since the fall of man there has been in all creation an aspiration for revival (Rom. 8:19-23). Adam's fall brought corruption, slavery, and death into the whole creation (Rom. 5:12); everything is decaying and is under the slavery of corruption. All the things that are under this slavery aspire to be revived.

The universal need for revival, for restoration, can be met only by Christ and in Christ. Only Christ, who was resurrected on the third day (1 Cor. 15:4), is the renewing power. For the whole universe and for all mankind, Christ is the reality of the third day (John 11:25). The reality of the third day is the person of the resurrected Christ with the reality of revival. Christ, therefore, is the element of the revival for which all creation aspires. The corruption and desolation can be swallowed up only by Christ's resurrection. The way to experience revival is to contact Christ by repenting and confessing our sins, failures, and darkness, thereby entering into Him as the resurrection. (Hab. 3:2, footnote 1)

Today's Reading

[As a conclusion] to the life-study of the Minor Prophets, I have the burden to speak a word concerning the revival revealed in the Minor Prophets. We may say that this matter of revival is the "kernel" within the "shell" of the books of the Minor Prophets.

Habakkuk 3:2a speaks of revival....Among God's elect there has always been an aspiration to be revived. As long as you are a saved one, every day, consciously or unconsciously, there is an

241

aspiration with a spontaneous prayer within you: "O Lord, revive us." Although we may not realize it, such an aspiration has been within us through all the years of our Christian life. We may think that Habakkuk's prayer for revival was good for him but has nothing to do with us. However, regarding his prayer, we need to realize that with God there is no time element. In the eyes of God, one person among His elect represents the whole. God always considers His elect as a corporate Body. This means that Habakkuk and we are one in the unit of God's elect. Thus, when Habakkuk prayed for revival, we also prayed. We prayed for revival twenty-six hundred years ago. Such a prayer is an everlasting prayer.

I [have] charged the saints to put the God-ordained way into a living practice, but without a revival, how could we have anything living? If we endeavor to practice just the first step of the God-ordained way—to visit people for the gospel—without being revived, this will be a heavy burden that no one can bear. We all need to realize that we have been saved and kept on earth to do one thing—to go to disciple the nations, beginning from "Jerusalem" and spreading to "Judea," to "Samaria," and to the uttermost part of the earth (Acts 1:8). If we live for our education, a career, a good marriage, or a nice house, that is vanity of vanities. We are living here for the spreading of the Lord Jesus, not merely to our neighborhood but to the entire world. If we would do this, we need to be revived. This is why the Lord has led us to practice the morning revival.

This matter of morning revival is according to the natural law in God's creation. God created the universe so that there is a sunrising every twenty-four hours. We believers should follow the sunrising to be revived every morning. Every day we need a "sunrising," and this sunrising is a revival. If we experience a daily revival, then we will be living and qualified to practice the God-ordained way and to help the church to take this way. (*Life-study of Malachi*, pp. 19-20)

Further Reading: Life-study of Malachi, msg. 4

Enlightenment and inspiration: _____

_____

_____

Morning Nourishment

Hosea For the children of Israel will abide for many days
3:4 without king and without prince and without sacrifice
and without pillar and without ephod and teraphim.
6:1-2 **Come and let us return to Jehovah; for He has torn
us, but He will heal us, and He has stricken *us*, but
He will bind us up. He will enliven us after two
days; on the third day He will raise us up, and we
will live in His presence.**

In Hosea 6:1 we have a word concerning Israel's coming and re-turning to Jehovah....Verse 2 says, "He will enliven us after two days; / On the third day He will raise us up...." What are the "two days," and what is "the third day" in this verse? In the Bible there is a principle that "with the Lord one day is like a thousand years" (2 Pet. 3:8). According to this principle, the two days here might signify the first two periods of a thousand years each, counting from A.D. 70, when the Roman prince Titus destroyed Jerusalem and the temple, cruelly killed thousands of Jews, and scattered the Jews among the nations. From that time the Jews have been without king, without prince, without sacrifice, and without the temple, fulfilling Hosea's prophecy in 3:4. For two thousand years God has left Israel in a dead condition. After this two-thousand-year period, the third thousand years will come. The third day in 6:2 might signify the third period of a thousand years, that is, the millennium, the age of restoration, in the reality of Christ's resurrection (Rev. 20:4, 6). (*Life-study of Hosea,* pp. 33-34)

Today's Reading

In Hosea 6:3 there is a word concerning knowing Jehovah and concerning Christ's going forth as the dawn and His coming as the rain. The first part of the verse says, "Therefore let us know, let us pursue knowing Jehovah." The remainder of the verse says that Christ's going forth is as sure as the dawn. He will come to us as the rain, as the late rain which waters the earth (in the restoration of the millennium—Matt. 19:28; Rev. 20:4, 6).

In Hosea 6:11 we have Jehovah's promise to Judah in the return of the apostate people. This promise is that there will be a harvest appointed for Judah, when Jehovah will turn the captivity of His people. This means that in the restoration all the Israelites, including the northern kingdom of Israel and the southern kingdom of Judah, will be very rich in all kinds of produce from the earth. The earth was created by God to produce a rich harvest, but due to the fall of man, the earth was cursed to grow thorns, and man has had to labor with sweat for food (Gen. 3:17-19). In the restoration time the earth will be restored to its original condition and will be rich, fertile, and productive. Thus, a harvest will be apportioned to Judah for their enjoyment. (*Life-study of Hosea,* p. 34)

On the one hand, Habakkuk prayed for revival; on the other hand, Hosea spoke of the desolation of the "two days" and the resurrection on the "third day": "He will enliven us after two days; / On the third day He will raise us up" (6:2). Since to God a thousand years are as one day (2 Pet. 3:8), these "two days" may refer to a period of two thousand years. For almost two thousand years, from the time Titus destroyed Jerusalem and the temple in A.D. 70, Israel, our representative, has been desolate. From that year Israel lost the priesthood, the sacrifices, the prophets, the king, and the temple. Eventually, there will be the "third day"—the thousand years of the millennial kingdom—when Israel will be raised up, that is, restored.

The principle is the same in our Christian life. At a certain time we became desolate. After the two days of desolation, there is the third day, which signifies the pneumatic Christ in resurrection. Today we may receive the pneumatic Christ in resurrection and thus enjoy the reality of His resurrection. If we have the resurrected Christ, we are in the morning, the sunrising, and this is a real revival to us. In 1984 I realized that the recovery was in a dormant condition, like the desolation of the two days in Hosea 6:2. However, if we experience a real revival, we will be in the third day. (*Life-study of Malachi,* pp. 20-21)

Further Reading: Life-study of Hosea, msg. 4

Enlightenment and inspiration: _____

_____

_____

Morning Nourishment

Rom. For we know that the whole creation groans to-
8:22-23 gether and travails in pain together until now. And
        not only *so*, but we ourselves also, who have the
        firstfruits of the Spirit, even we ourselves groan in
        ourselves, eagerly awaiting sonship, the redemp-
        tion of our body.

John ...I am the resurrection and the life; he who be-
11:25 lieves into Me, even if he should die, shall live.

The revival revealed in the Minor Prophets can be applied to
the family, to the church, to the nations, to the entire human
race, and even to the whole universe. In principle, everything
and everyone on earth are in the desolation of the two days spoken of in Hosea 6:2.

Since the fall of man, there has been in all of creation an aspiration for revival. Concerning this, Romans 8:20-22 says, "The
creation was made subject to vanity, not of its own will, but
because of Him who subjected it, in hope that the creation itself
will also be freed from the slavery of corruption into the freedom
of the glory of the children of God. For we know that the whole
creation groans together and travails in pain together until
now." As a result of Adam's fall, corruption, slavery, and death
have come into the whole creation. Today everything is decaying
and is under the slavery of corruption. All the things that are
under this slavery aspire to be revived. (*Life-study of Malachi,*
pp. 23-24)

Today's Reading

Man's fall brought in corruption, and with corruption there is
slavery. Because of this corruption and slavery, there is the need
everywhere for revival, for restoration. This need can be met
only by Christ and in Christ. Christ was resurrected on the third
day, and as the pneumatic Christ in resurrection, He is the reality of the third day. Christ, therefore, is the element of the revival
for which all of creation aspires. The corruption and desolation

can be swallowed up only by Christ's resurrection.

Unbelievers as well as believers aspire to be revived, to have a new beginning. Everyone wants something new. Only Christ is the renewing factor. Only Christ, who rose up on the third day, is the renewing power. For the whole universe and for all of mankind, Christ is the reality of the third day.

When we received Christ, we received Him as the One who is Himself the resurrection (John 11:25). Immediately after receiving Him, we had a new beginning in our human life. That new beginning was a revival. However, eventually we again entered into a state of desolation and thus needed another revival. This cycle of desolation and revival, revival and desolation, has been repeated again and again.

The way to have the revival we need is to contact Christ, repenting and confessing our sins, failures, and darkness. By doing this we are brought from the desolation of the two days to the resurrection of the third day. Whenever we are in desolation we need such a revival. We need to come to the third day, and the third day is nothing other than the person of the resurrected Christ with the reality of revival. In addition, we have the outpouring of the Triune God as the consummated, all-inclusive, life-giving Spirit, and our spirit responds by being stirred up.

When our spirit is stirred up in response to the outpouring of the Spirit, we enjoy Christ not only as the resurrected One but also as the One desired by all of mankind. He is mankind's unique need. Everyone, the believers and the unbelievers alike, desires Christ.

The Christ we desire has enacted the new covenant and He, as its surety, is now executing it. Through this covenant God has been allotted to us as our legal portion in Christ, who is the Sun of righteousness with healing in His wings. Apart from Him, we have darkness and unrighteousness, but with Him everything is light and righteousness. (*Life-study of Malachi*, pp. 24-25)

Further Reading: Life-study of 1 & 2 Chronicles, msg. 2

Enlightenment and inspiration: ___Vevival = new___
___beginning something new___
___Only X is the renewing factor/power.___

Morning Nourishment

Joel ...I will pour out My Spirit upon all flesh, and your
2:28-29 sons and your daughters shall prophesy; your old
men shall dream dreams; your young men shall see
visions....In those days I will pour out My Spirit.
Hag. ...Jehovah stirred up the spirit of Zerubbabel...and
1:14 the spirit of Joshua...the high priest, and the spirit
of all the remnant of the people; and they came and
did work in the house of Jehovah of hosts their God.

Joel 2:28 and 29 speak of the outpouring of the Spirit. Every day
we need the outpouring of the all-inclusive, consummated, compound, life-giving Spirit as the processed and consummated Triune God. This all-inclusive Spirit includes Christ's divinity and
humanity, the effectiveness of His death, and the power of His
resurrection. This Spirit is our portion, our inheritance. (*Life-
study of Malachi*, p. 21)

Today's Reading

[In Haggai 1:14] we see the response of God's elect, who were
stirred up by the Lord in the order of God's authority. When they
responded by being stirred up in their spirit by the Lord, we all
were included.

In the Minor Prophets there are both the divine Spirit, the
consummated Spirit of God, and the human spirit, the stirred-
up spirit of God's elect. The divine Spirit has been poured out,
and our human spirit (the key to experiencing and enjoying
Christ) responds to such a Spirit by being stirred up.

We may feel that our spirit was stirred up early in our Christian life but that it is no longer stirred up. However, this is not
true. Unconsciously, the spirit of every regenerated believer is
stirred up. If we go to a place of worldly entertainment, our spirit
will be stirred up to tell us to leave that place. Whenever we grieve
the Spirit (Eph. 4:30), we have no peace. This is the stirring up of
our spirit. When we read the Bible, we feel calm and peaceful.
Even in this calmness, our spirit is under the stirring up by the

Spirit. Every day we cannot avoid the stirring up of our spirit. The Bible reveals that once the consummated, compound, life-giving Spirit comes into us, He will never leave. As He dwells in us, He is often a "troublemaker," stirring us up either negatively or positively. If we take care of this negative or positive stirring up, we will be revived, and we will be strengthened and encouraged to carry out the God-ordained way....The Minor Prophets also reveal that God's Christ is our enjoyment. The enjoyment of God's Christ is actually the enjoyment of God Himself....We may enjoy Christ as the Desire of God's elect (Mal. 3:1b; cf. Hag. 2:7a). Whether we are hot or cold toward the Lord, we desire Christ. Can you say that you have no desire for Christ? Every day we desire Christ....We may enjoy Christ also as the Angel of the covenant (Mal. 3:1b). For Him to be the Angel means that He is a serving one. In His coming back, Christ will be the Angel of the covenant. He enacted the new covenant with His blood at His table (Matt. 26:26-29; Luke 22:20). In the new covenant, God is imparted into us as life and as our life supply, and we have the forgiveness of sins (Jer. 31:31-34)....Christ not only enacted the new covenant through His death, but in resurrection He executes the new covenant as its surety (Heb. 7:22), making it real to us. In particular, He assures us that our sins have been forgiven and that we have Him as our life and life supply signified by the bread at the Lord's table. Day by day we may enjoy Him as the surety of the new covenant....As the Angel of the covenant, Christ dispenses the riches of the covenanted Triune God into His elect. According to Acts 26:18b, we have received not only the forgiveness of sins but also "an inheritance among those who have been sanctified." This inheritance is the Triune God Himself with all He has, all He has done, and all He will do for His redeemed people. The Triune God is embodied in the all-inclusive Christ, who is "the allotted portion of the saints" as their inheritance (Col. 1:12). (*Life-study of Malachi*, pp. 21-23)

Further Reading: Life-study of Malachi, msg. 4

Enlightenment and inspiration: _____

_____

_____

_____

Morning Nourishment

Mal. But unto you who fear My name will the Sun of
4:2 righteousness arise with healing in His wings, and
you will go forth and leap about like well-fed calves.
Rev. And I saw, and behold, the Lamb standing on
14:1 Mount Zion, and with Him a hundred and forty-
four thousand, having His name and the name of
His Father written on their foreheads.

Malachi 4:2 tells us that we may enjoy Christ as the Sun of
righteousness with healing in His wings....As the Sun of righteousness, Christ is our enjoyment for growing in life, in the
dispelling of the darkness. Just as the shining of the sunlight
enables plants to grow, Christ's shining as the Sun of righteousness is for our growth in life....As the Sun of righteousness,
Christ is our enjoyment also for healing in life, in the effacing of
unrighteousness. Before we enjoy this healing in life, unrighteousness prevails, but through this healing unrighteousness is
effaced and is replaced by righteousness.

When we have such a Christ, we not only have revival—we
have restoration. The millennial kingdom will be a time of restoration. This restoration will consummate in the new heaven and
new earth with the New Jerusalem as the center. That will be
the ultimate, the consummate, restoration accomplished by the
resurrected Christ. (*Life-study of Malachi*, pp. 23, 25)

Today's Reading

It is a great miracle and a deep mystery that God has a way to
be joined to man and mingled with man. God became man that
man may become God. Such an economy is incomprehensible to
both angels and man. This economy is of God's desire, and it will
reach, attain, the high peak of God's goal. Ultimately the holy city,
Jerusalem, will be the aggregate of all the visions and revelations
throughout the Scriptures. The Triune God and the tripartite man
will become a loving couple in eternity as man yet still God. Divinity
and humanity will become a mutual abode, and the glory of God will
be expressed in humanity radiantly in splendor to the uttermost.

I hope that the saints in all the churches throughout the earth, especially the co-workers and the elders, will see this revelation and then rise up to pray that God would give us a new revival—a revival which has never been recorded in history.

In God's view *mankind* is a negative term referring to fallen man. As believers in Christ and children of God, we are not mankind—we are God-man kind. To realize this is to be changed, even revolutionized. When we realize that we are God-men, we will say, "Lord, You are the first God-man, and we are the many God-men following You. You lived a human life, not by Your human life but by God's divine life to express Him....Lord, You are my life today and You are my person. You are just me. I therefore must die. I need to be conformed to Your death. I have to be crucified to die every day to live a God-man's life, a human life yet not by my human life but by the divine life, with Your life and Your nature as my constitution to express You in Your divine attributes, which become my human virtues." This makes us not just a Christian or a believer in Christ but a God-man, one kind with God. This is the highest point of God's gospel.

According to this gospel we were fallen, yet Christ died for us. If we believe in Him and receive Him, we will have the eternal life to be the sons of God....At the end of this age, we are teaching and preaching the truth that God became a man in order to make man God, the same as He is in life and in nature but not in the Godhead. It is a great blessing to hear this truth.

After hearing that God wants a group of God-men, how can you be content to be anything else?...Do you want to be a typical Chinese or a typical American? Do you want to be merely a Christian or a believer in Christ? We should all declare that we want to live the life of a God-man. Eventually, the God-men will be the victors, the overcomers, the Zion within Jerusalem. This will bring in a new revival which has never been seen in history, and this will end this age. (*Life-study of 1 & 2 Chronicles,* pp. 15, 27-28)

Further Reading: Life-study of 1 & 2 Chronicles, msg. 4

Enlightenment and inspiration: _____

_____
_____
_____

Morning Nourishment

John ...Jesus said..., Simon,...do you love Me...? He said to
21:15-17 Him, Yes, Lord, You know that I love You. He said to
him, Feed My lambs. He said to him again a second
time, Simon,...do you love Me?...Shepherd My sheep.
He said to him the third time, Simon,...do you love
Me?...Feed My sheep.

The Lord's shepherding was firstly in His earthly ministry
(Matt. 9:36). The Lord saw the Israelites as sheep harassed by
their leaders; they were cast away like sheep not having a shepherd. The Lord as the Shepherd of God's elect prayed, and God
told His sent One to appoint twelve apostles that they might
take care of the sheep of God (Matt. 10:1-6).

The Lord's shepherding is secondly in His heavenly ministry
(1 Pet. 5:4) to take care of the church of God, issuing in His Body.
When He was on the earth, He was shepherding. After His resurrection and ascension to the heavens, He is still shepherding.

When the Lord stayed with His disciples after His resurrection and before His ascension, in one of His appearings, He com-
missioned Peter to feed His lambs and shepherd His sheep in
His absence, while He is in the heavens (John 21:15-17). Shepherding implies feeding, but it includes much more than feeding.
To shepherd is to take all-inclusive tender care of the flock.
(*Crystallization-study of the Gospel of John,* pp. 130-131)

Today's Reading

We have to follow the steps of the processed Triune God in His
seeking and gaining fallen people. Luke 15 records that the Pharisees and scribes criticized the Lord...(v. 2). Then the Lord told
three wonderful parables, which unveil the saving love of the Triune God toward sinners....The Son as the shepherd would leave
the ninety-nine to seek the one lost sheep (Luke 15:3-7)....The
second parable...of a woman seeking a lost coin (vv. 8-10)...signi-
fies the Spirit seeking a lost sinner. The Son's finding took place
outside the sinner and was completed at the cross through His re-
demptive death. The Spirit's seeking is inward and is carried out

by His working within the repenting sinner.

Because of the Son's step of seeking the sinner by dying on the cross and the Spirit's step of sanctifying by searching and cleansing the sinner's inward parts, the sinner comes to his senses. This is shown by the prodigal son's coming to himself and desiring to return to his father (vv. 17-18)....The sinner is awakened by the Spirit's seeking to cause him to return to the Father.

I hope that there will be a genuine revival among us by our receiving this burden of shepherding. If all the churches receive this teaching to participate in Christ's wonderful shepherding, there will be a big revival in the recovery. In the past we did much speaking and teaching with very little shepherding. Shepherding and teaching should be like two feet for our move with the Lord. Our shepherding should always be with teaching, and our teaching should always be with shepherding.

John 21...reveals the apostolic ministry in cooperation with Christ's heavenly ministry. In His heavenly ministry Christ is shepherding people, and we need to cooperate with Him by shepherding people. Without shepherding, our work for the Lord cannot be effective. We must learn all the truths so that we may have something to speak and go to contact people to shepherd them.

Shepherding is something divine. In order to be a shepherd, we must be a witness of Christ, a member of Christ, and a brother of Christ, sharing His sonship. Then we will participate in the oracle of the sonship to become a prophet. As a prophet for God's oracle, we will speak for the Lord. Meanwhile, we need to shepherd people. This is the way to be fruitful, to have the multiplication and the increase. If this kind of fellowship is received by us, I believe there will be a big revival on the earth, not by a few spiritual giants but by the many members of Christ's Body being shepherds who follow the steps of the processed Triune God in seeking and gaining fallen people. (*The Vital Groups,* pp. 39-40)

Further Reading: The Vital Groups, msg. 4; *Crystallization-study of the Gospel of John,* msg. 13

Enlightenment and inspiration: _____

_____

_____

_____

What Miracle! What Mystery!

1   What miracle! What mystery!
    That God and man should blended be!
    God became man to make man God,
    Untraceable economy!
    From His good pleasure, heart's desire,
    His highest goal attained will be.

2   Flesh He became, the first God-man,
    His pleasure that I God may be:
    In life and nature I'm God's kind,
    Though Godhead's His exclusively.
    His attributes my virtues are;
    His glorious image shines through me.

3   No longer I alone that live,
    But God together lives with me.
    Built with the saints in the Triune God,
    His universal house we'll be,
    And His organic Body we
    For His expression corp'rately.

4   Jerusalem, the ultimate,
    Of visions the totality;
    The Triune God, tripartite man—
    A loving pair eternally—
    As man yet God they coinhere,
    A mutual dwelling place to be;
    God's glory in humanity
    Shines forth in splendor radiantly!

Composition for prophecy with main point and sub-points:

Reading Schedule for the Recovery Version of the Old Testament with Footnotes

Wk.	Lord's Day	Monday	Tuesday	Wednesday	Thursday	Friday	Saturday
1	Gen 1:1-5 ☐	1:6-23 ☐	1:24-31 ☐	2:1-9 ☐	2:10-25 ☐	3:1-13 ☐	3:14-24 ☐
2	4:1-26 ☐	5:1-32 ☐	6:1-22 ☐	7:1—8:3 ☐	8:4-22 ☐	9:1-29 ☐	10:1-32 ☐
3	11:1-32 ☐	12:1-20 ☐	13:1-18 ☐	14:1-24 ☐	15:1-21 ☐	16:1-16 ☐	17:1-27 ☐
4	18:1-33 ☐	19:1-38 ☐	20:1-18 ☐	21:1-34 ☐	22:1-24 ☐	23:1—24:27 ☐	24:28-67 ☐
5	25:1-34 ☐	26:1-35 ☐	27:1-46 ☐	28:1-22 ☐	29:1-35 ☐	30:1-43 ☐	31:1-55 ☐
6	32:1-32 ☐	33:1—34:31 ☐	35:1-29 ☐	36:1-43 ☐	37:1-36 ☐	38:1—39:23 ☐	40:1—41:13 ☐
7	41:14-57 ☐	42:1-38 ☐	43:1-34 ☐	44:1-34 ☐	45:1-28 ☐	46:1-34 ☐	47:1-31 ☐
8	48:1-22 ☐	49:1-15 ☐	49:16-33 ☐	50:1-26 ☐	Exo 1:1-22 ☐	2:1-25 ☐	3:1-22 ☐
9	4:1-31 ☐	5:1-23 ☐	6:1-30 ☐	7:1-25 ☐	8:1-32 ☐	9:1-35 ☐	10:1-29 ☐
10	11:1-10 ☐	12:1-14 ☐	12:15-36 ☐	12:37-51 ☐	13:1-22 ☐	14:1-31 ☐	15:1-27 ☐
11	16:1-36 ☐	17:1-16 ☐	18:1-27 ☐	19:1-25 ☐	20:1-26 ☐	21:1-36 ☐	22:1-31 ☐
12	23:1-33 ☐	24:1-18 ☐	25:1-22 ☐	25:23-40 ☐	26:1-14 ☐	26:15-37 ☐	27:1-21 ☐
13	28:1-21 ☐	28:22-43 ☐	29:1-21 ☐	29:22-46 ☐	30:1-10 ☐	30:11-38 ☐	31:1-17 ☐
14	31:18—32:35 ☐	33:1-23 ☐	34:1-35 ☐	35:1-35 ☐	36:1-38 ☐	37:1-29 ☐	38:1-31 ☐
15	39:1-43 ☐	40:1-38 ☐	Lev 1:1-17 ☐	2:1-16 ☐	3:1-17 ☐	4:1-35 ☐	5:1-19 ☐
16	6:1-30 ☐	7:1-38 ☐	8:1-36 ☐	9:1-24 ☐	10:1-20 ☐	11:1-47 ☐	12:1-8 ☐
17	13:1-28 ☐	13:29-59 ☐	14:1-18 ☐	14:19-32 ☐	14:33-57 ☐	15:1-33 ☐	16:1-17 ☐
18	16:18-34 ☐	17:1-16 ☐	18:1-30 ☐	19:1-37 ☐	20:1-27 ☐	21:1-24 ☐	22:1-33 ☐
19	23:1-22 ☐	23:23-44 ☐	24:1-23 ☐	25:1-23 ☐	25:24-55 ☐	26:1-24 ☐	26:25-46 ☐
20	27:1-34 ☐	Num 1:1-54 ☐	2:1-34 ☐	3:1-51 ☐	4:1-49 ☐	5:1-31 ☐	6:1-27 ☐
21	7:1-41 ☐	7:42-88 ☐	7:89—8:26 ☐	9:1-23 ☐	10:1-36 ☐	11:1-35 ☐	12:1—13:33 ☐
22	14:1-45 ☐	15:1-41 ☐	16:1-50 ☐	17:1—18:7 ☐	18:8-32 ☐	19:1-22 ☐	20:1-29 ☐
23	21:1-35 ☐	22:1-41 ☐	23:1-30 ☐	24:1-25 ☐	25:1-18 ☐	26:1-65 ☐	27:1-23 ☐
24	28:1-31 ☐	29:1-40 ☐	30:1—31:24 ☐	31:25-54 ☐	32:1-42 ☐	33:1-56 ☐	34:1-29 ☐
25	35:1-34 ☐	36:1-13 ☐	Deut 1:1-46 ☐	2:1-37 ☐	3:1-29 ☐	4:1-49 ☐	5:1-33 ☐
26	6:1—7:26 ☐	8:1-20 ☐	9:1-29 ☐	10:1-22 ☐	11:1-32 ☐	12:1-32 ☐	13:1—14:21 ☐

Reading Schedule for the Recovery Version of the Old Testament with Footnotes

Wk.	Lord's Day	Monday	Tuesday	Wednesday	Thursday	Friday	Saturday
27	☐ 14:22—15:23	☐ 16:1-22	☐ 17:1—18:8	☐ 18:9—19:21	☐ 20:1—21:17	☐ 21:18—22:30	☐ 23:1-25
28	☐ 24:1-22	☐ 25:1-19	☐ 26:1-19	☐ 27:1-26	☐ 28:1-68	☐ 29:1-29	☐ 30:1—31:29
29	☐ 31:30—32:52	☐ 33:1-29	☐ 34:1-12	☐ Josh 1:1-18	☐ 2:1-24	☐ 3:1-17	☐ 4:1-24
30	☐ 5:1-15	☐ 6:1-27	☐ 7:1-26	☐ 8:1-35	☐ 9:1-27	☐ 10:1-43	☐ 11:1—12:24
31	☐ 13:1-33	☐ 14:1—15:63	☐ 16:1—18:28	☐ 19:1-51	☐ 20:1—21:45	☐ 22:1-34	☐ 23:1—24:33
32	☐ Judg 1:1-36	☐ 2:1-23	☐ 3:1-31	☐ 4:1-24	☐ 5:1-31	☐ 6:1-40	☐ 7:1-25
33	☐ 8:1-35	☐ 9:1-57	☐ 10:1—11:40	☐ 12:1—13:25	☐ 14:1—15:20	☐ 16:1-31	☐ 17:1—18:31
34	☐ 19:1-30	☐ 20:1-48	☐ 21:1-25	☐ Ruth 1:1-22	☐ 2:1-23	☐ 3:1-18	☐ 4:1-22
35	☐ 1 Sam 1:1-28	☐ 2:1-36	☐ 3:1—4:22	☐ 5:1—6:21	☐ 7:1—8:22	☐ 9:1-27	☐ 10:1—11:15
36	☐ 12:1—13:23	☐ 14:1-52	☐ 15:1-35	☐ 16:1-23	☐ 17:1-58	☐ 18:1-30	☐ 19:1-24
37	☐ 20:1-42	☐ 21:1—22:23	☐ 23:1—24:22	☐ 25:1-44	☐ 26:1-25	☐ 27:1—28:25	☐ 29:1—30:31
38	☐ 31:1-13	☐ 2 Sam 1:1-27	☐ 2:1-32	☐ 3:1-39	☐ 4:1—5:25	☐ 6:1-23	☐ 7:1-29
39	☐ 8:1—9:13	☐ 10:1—11:27	☐ 12:1-31	☐ 13:1-39	☐ 14:1-33	☐ 15:1—16:23	☐ 17:1—18:33
40	☐ 19:1-43	☐ 20:1—21:22	☐ 22:1-51	☐ 23:1-39	☐ 24:1-25	☐ 1 Kings 1:1-19	☐ 1:20-53
41	☐ 2:1-46	☐ 3:1-28	☐ 4:1-34	☐ 5:1—6:38	☐ 7:1-22	☐ 7:23-51	☐ 8:1-36
42	☐ 8:37-66	☐ 9:1-28	☐ 10:1-29	☐ 11:1-43	☐ 12:1-33	☐ 13:1-34	☐ 14:1-31
43	☐ 15:1-34	☐ 16:1—17:24	☐ 18:1-46	☐ 19:1-21	☐ 20:1-43	☐ 21:1—22:53	☐ 2 Kings 1:1-18
44	☐ 2:1—3:27	☐ 4:1-44	☐ 5:1—6:33	☐ 7:1-20	☐ 8:1-29	☐ 9:1-37	☐ 10:1-36
45	☐ 11:1—12:21	☐ 13:1—14:29	☐ 15:1-38	☐ 16:1-20	☐ 17:1-41	☐ 18:1-37	☐ 19:1-37
46	☐ 20:1—21:26	☐ 22:1-20	☐ 23:1-37	☐ 24:1—25:30	☐ 1 Chron 1:1-54	☐ 2:1—3:24	☐ 4:1—5:26
47	☐ 6:1-81	☐ 7:1-40	☐ 8:1-40	☐ 9:1-44	☐ 10:1—11:47	☐ 12:1-40	☐ 13:1—14:17
48	☐ 15:1—16:43	☐ 17:1-27	☐ 18:1—19:19	☐ 20:1—21:30	☐ 22:1—23:32	☐ 24:1—25:31	☐ 26:1-32
49	☐ 27:1-34	☐ 28:1—29:30	☐ 2 Chron 1:1-17	☐ 2:1—3:17	☐ 4:1—5:14	☐ 6:1-42	☐ 7:1—8:18
50	☐ 9:1—10:19	☐ 11:1—12:16	☐ 13:1—15:19	☐ 16:1—17:19	☐ 18:1—19:11	☐ 20:1-37	☐ 21:1—22:12
51	☐ 23:1—24:27	☐ 25:1—26:23	☐ 27:1—28:27	☐ 29:1-36	☐ 30:1—31:21	☐ 32:1-33	☐ 33:1—34:33
52	☐ 35:1—36:23	☐ Ezra 1:1-11	☐ 2:1-70	☐ 3:1—4:24	☐ 5:1—6:22	☐ 7:1-28	☐ 8:1-36

Reading Schedule for the Recovery Version of the Old Testament with Footnotes

Wk.	Lord's Day	Monday	Tuesday	Wednesday	Thursday	Friday	Saturday
53	☐ 9:1—10:44	☐ Neh 1:1-11	☐ 2:1—3:32	☐ 4:1—5:19	☐ 6:1-19	☐ 7:1-73	☐ 8:1-18
54	☐ 9:1-20	☐ 9:21-38	☐ 10:1—11:36	☐ 12:1-47	☐ 13:1-31	☐ Esth 1:1-22	☐ 2:1—3:15
55	☐ 4:1—5:14	☐ 6:1—7:10	☐ 8:1-17	☐ 9:1—10:3	☐ Job 1:1-22	☐ 2:1—3:26	☐ 4:1—5:27
56	☐ 6:1—7:21	☐ 8:1—9:35	☐ 10:1—11:20	☐ 12:1—13:28	☐ 14:1—15:35	☐ 16:1—17:16	☐ 18:1—19:29
57	☐ 20:1—21:34	☐ 22:1—23:17	☐ 24:1—25:6	☐ 26:1—27:23	☐ 28:1—29:25	☐ 30:1—31:40	☐ 32:1—33:33
58	☐ 34:1—35:16	☐ 36:1-33	☐ 37:1-24	☐ 38:1-41	☐ 39:1-30	☐ 40:1-24	☐ 41:1-34
59	☐ 42:1-17	☐ Psa 1:1-6	☐ 2:1—3:8	☐ 4:1—6:10	☐ 7:1—8:9	☐ 9:1—10:18	☐ 11:1—15:5
60	☐ 16:1—17:15	☐ 18:1-50	☐ 19:1—21:13	☐ 22:1-31	☐ 23:1—24:10	☐ 25:1—27:14	☐ 28:1—30:12
61	☐ 31:1—32:11	☐ 33:1—34:22	☐ 35:1—36:12	☐ 37:1-40	☐ 38:1—39:13	☐ 40:1—41:13	☐ 42:1—43:5
62	☐ 44:1-26	☐ 45:1-17	☐ 46:1—48:14	☐ 49:1—50:23	☐ 51:1—52:9	☐ 53:1—55:23	☐ 56:1—58:11
63	☐ 59:1—61:8	☐ 62:1—64:10	☐ 65:1—67:7	☐ 68:1-35	☐ 69:1—70:5	☐ 71:1—72:20	☐ 73:1—74:23
64	☐ 75:1—77:20	☐ 78:1-72	☐ 79:1—81:16	☐ 82:1—84:12	☐ 85:1—87:7	☐ 88:1—89:52	☐ 90:1—91:16
65	☐ 92:1—94:23	☐ 95:1—97:12	☐ 98:1—101:8	☐ 102:1—103:22	☐ 104:1—105:45	☐ 106:1-48	☐ 107:1-43
66	☐ 108:1—109:31	☐ 110:1—112:10	☐ 113:1—115:18	☐ 116:1—118:29	☐ 119:1-32	☐ 119:33-72	☐ 119:73-120
67	☐ 119:121-176	☐ 120:1—124:8	☐ 125:1—128:6	☐ 129:1—132:18	☐ 133:1—135:21	☐ 136:1—138:8	☐ 139:1—140:13
68	☐ 141:1—144:15	☐ 145:1—147:20	☐ 148:1—150:6	☐ Prov 1:1-33	☐ 2:1—3:35	☐ 4:1—5:23	☐ 6:1-35
69	☐ 7:1—8:36	☐ 9:1—10:32	☐ 11:1—12:28	☐ 13:1—14:35	☐ 15:1-33	☐ 16:1-33	☐ 17:1-28
70	☐ 18:1-24	☐ 19:1—20:30	☐ 21:1—22:29	☐ 23:1-35	☐ 24:1—25:28	☐ 26:1—27:27	☐ 28:1—29:27
71	☐ 30:1-33	☐ 31:1-31	☐ Eccl 1:1-18	☐ 2:1—3:22	☐ 4:1—5:20	☐ 6:1—7:29	☐ 8:1—9:18
72	☐ 10:1—11:10	☐ 12:1-14	☐ S.S 1:1-8	☐ 1:9-17	☐ 2:1-17	☐ 3:1-11	☐ 4:1-8
73	☐ 4:9-16	☐ 5:1-16	☐ 6:1-13	☐ 7:1-13	☐ 8:1-14	☐ Isa 1:1-11	☐ 1:12-31
74	☐ 2:1-22	☐ 3:1-26	☐ 4:1-6	☐ 5:1-30	☐ 6:1-13	☐ 7:1-25	☐ 8:1-22
75	☐ 9:1-21	☐ 10:1-34	☐ 11:1—12:6	☐ 13:1-22	☐ 14:1-14	☐ 14:15-32	☐ 15:1—16:14
76	☐ 17:1—18:7	☐ 19:1-25	☐ 20:1—21:17	☐ 22:1-25	☐ 23:1-18	☐ 24:1-23	☐ 25:1-12
77	☐ 26:1-21	☐ 27:1-13	☐ 28:1-29	☐ 29:1-24	☐ 30:1-33	☐ 31:1—32:20	☐ 33:1-24
78	☐ 34:1-17	☐ 35:1-10	☐ 36:1-22	☐ 37:1-38	☐ 38:1—39:8	☐ 40:1-31	☐ 41:1-29

Reading Schedule for the Recovery Version of the Old Testament with Footnotes

Wk.	Lord's Day	Monday	Tuesday	Wednesday	Thursday	Friday	Saturday
79	☐ 42:1-25	☐ 43:1-28	☐ 44:1-28	☐ 45:1-25	☐ 46:1-13	☐ 47:1-15	☐ 48:1-22
80	☐ 49:1-13	☐ 49:14-26	☐ 50:1—51:23	☐ 52:1-15	☐ 53:1-12	☐ 54:1-17	☐ 55:1-13
81	☐ 56:1-12	☐ 57:1-21	☐ 58:1-14	☐ 59:1-21	☐ 60:1-22	☐ 61:1-11	☐ 62:1-12
82	☐ 63:1-19	☐ 64:1-12	☐ 65:1-25	☐ 66:1-24	☐ Jer 1:1-19	☐ 2:1-19	☐ 2:20-37
83	☐ 3:1-25	☐ 4:1-31	☐ 5:1-31	☐ 6:1-30	☐ 7:1-34	☐ 8:1-22	☐ 9:1-26
84	☐ 10:1-25	☐ 11:1—12:17	☐ 13:1-27	☐ 14:1-22	☐ 15:1-21	☐ 16:1—17:27	☐ 18:1-23
85	☐ 19:1—20:18	☐ 21:1—22:30	☐ 23:1-40	☐ 24:1—25:38	☐ 26:1—27:22	☐ 28:1—29:32	☐ 30:1-24
86	☐ 31:1-23	☐ 31:24-40	☐ 32:1-44	☐ 33:1-26	☐ 34:1-22	☐ 35:1-19	☐ 36:1-32
87	☐ 37:1-21	☐ 38:1-28	☐ 39:1—40:16	☐ 41:1—42:22	☐ 43:1—44:30	☐ 45:1—46:28	☐ 47:1—48:16
88	☐ 48:17-47	☐ 49:1-22	☐ 49:23-39	☐ 50:1-27	☐ 50:28-46	☐ 51:1-27	☐ 51:28-64
89	☐ 52:1-34	☐ Lam 1:1-22	☐ 2:1-22	☐ 3:1-39	☐ 3:40-66	☐ 4:1-22	☐ 5:1-22
90	☐ Ezek 1:1-14	☐ 1:15-28	☐ 2:1—3:27	☐ 4:1—5:17	☐ 6:1—7:27	☐ 8:1—9:11	☐ 10:1—11:25
91	☐ 12:1—13:23	☐ 14:1—15:8	☐ 16:1-63	☐ 17:1—18:32	☐ 19:1-14	☐ 20:1-49	☐ 21:1-32
92	☐ 22:1-31	☐ 23:1-49	☐ 24:1-27	☐ 25:1—26:21	☐ 27:1-36	☐ 28:1-26	☐ 29:1—30:26
93	☐ 31:1—32:32	☐ 33:1-33	☐ 34:1-31	☐ 35:1—36:21	☐ 36:22-38	☐ 37:1-28	☐ 38:1—39:29
94	☐ 40:1-27	☐ 40:28-49	☐ 41:1-26	☐ 42:1—43:27	☐ 44:1-31	☐ 45:1-25	☐ 46:1-24
95	☐ 47:1-23	☐ 48:1-35	☐ Dan 1:1-21	☐ 2:1-30	☐ 2:31-49	☐ 3:1-30	☐ 4:1-37
96	☐ 5:1-31	☐ 6:1-28	☐ 7:1-12	☐ 7:13-28	☐ 8:1-27	☐ 9:1-27	☐ 10:1-21
97	☐ 11:1-22	☐ 11:23-45	☐ 12:1-13	☐ Hosea 1:1-11	☐ 2:1-23	☐ 3:1—4:19	☐ 5:1-15
98	☐ 6:1-11	☐ 7:1-16	☐ 8:1-14	☐ 9:1-17	☐ 10:1-15	☐ 11:1-12	☐ 12:1-14
99	☐ 13:1—14:9	☐ Joel 1:1-20	☐ 2:1-16	☐ 2:17-32	☐ 3:1-21	☐ Amos 1:1-15	☐ 2:1-16
100	☐ 3:1-15	☐ 4:1—5:27	☐ 6:1—7:17	☐ 8:1—9:15	☐ Obad 1-21	☐ Jonah 1:1-17	☐ 2:1—4:11
101	☐ Micah 1:1-16	☐ 2:1—3:12	☐ 4:1—5:15	☐ 6:1—7:20	☐ Nahum 1:1-15	☐ 2:1—3:19	☐ Hab 1:1-17
102	☐ 2:1-20	☐ 3:1-19	☐ Zeph 1:1-18	☐ 2:1-15	☐ 3:1-20	☐ Hag 1:1-15	☐ 2:1-23
103	☐ Zech 1:1-21	☐ 2:1-13	☐ 3:1-10	☐ 4:1-14	☐ 5:1—6:15	☐ 7:1—8:23	☐ 9:1-17
104	☐ 10:1—11:17	☐ 12:1—13:9	☐ 14:1-21	☐ Mal 1:1-14	☐ 2:1-17	☐ 3:1-18	☐ 4:1-6

Reading Schedule for the Recovery Version of the New Testament with Footnotes

Wk.	Lord's Day	Monday	Tuesday	Wednesday	Thursday	Friday	Saturday
1	☐ Matt 1:1-2	☐ 1:3-7	☐ 1:8-17	☐ 1:18-25	☐ 2:1-23	☐ 3:1-6	☐ 3:7-17
2	☐ 4:1-11	☐ 4:12-25	☐ 5:1-4	☐ 5:5-12	☐ 5:13-20	☐ 5:21-26	☐ 5:27-48
3	☐ 6:1-8	☐ 6:9-18	☐ 6:19-34	☐ 7:1-12	☐ 7:13-29	☐ 8:1-13	☐ 8:14-22
4	☐ 8:23-34	☐ 9:1-13	☐ 9:14-17	☐ 9:18-34	☐ 9:35—10:5	☐ 10:6-25	☐ 10:26-42
5	☐ 11:1-15	☐ 11:16-30	☐ 12:1-14	☐ 12:15-32	☐ 12:33-42	☐ 12:43—13:2	☐ 13:3-12
6	☐ 13:13-30	☐ 13:31-43	☐ 13:44-58	☐ 14:1-13	☐ 14:14-21	☐ 14:22-36	☐ 15:1-20
7	☐ 15:21-31	☐ 15:32-39	☐ 16:1-12	☐ 16:13-20	☐ 16:21-28	☐ 17:1-13	☐ 17:14-27
8	☐ 18:1-14	☐ 18:15-22	☐ 18:23-35	☐ 19:1-15	☐ 19:16-30	☐ 20:1-16	☐ 20:17-34
9	☐ 21:1-11	☐ 21:12-22	☐ 21:23-32	☐ 21:33-46	☐ 22:1-22	☐ 22:23-33	☐ 22:34-46
10	☐ 23:1-12	☐ 23:13-39	☐ 24:1-14	☐ 24:15-31	☐ 24:32-51	☐ 25:1-13	☐ 25:14-30
11	☐ 25:31-46	☐ 26:1-16	☐ 26:17-35	☐ 26:36-46	☐ 26:47-64	☐ 26:65-75	☐ 27:1-26
12	☐ 27:27-44	☐ 27:45-56	☐ 27:57—28:15	☐ 28:16-20	☐ Mark 1:1	☐ 1:2-6	☐ 1:7-13
13	☐ 1:14-28	☐ 1:29-45	☐ 2:1-12	☐ 2:13-28	☐ 3:1-19	☐ 3:20-35	☐ 4:1-25
14	☐ 4:26-41	☐ 5:1-20	☐ 5:21-43	☐ 6:1-29	☐ 6:30-56	☐ 7:1-23	☐ 7:24-37
15	☐ 8:1-26	☐ 8:27—9:1	☐ 9:2-29	☐ 9:30-50	☐ 10:1-16	☐ 10:17-34	☐ 10:35-52
16	☐ 11:1-16	☐ 11:17-33	☐ 12:1-27	☐ 12:28-44	☐ 13:1-13	☐ 13:14-37	☐ 14:1-26
17	☐ 14:27-52	☐ 14:53-72	☐ 15:1-15	☐ 15:16-47	☐ 16:1-8	☐ 16:9-20	☐ Luke 1:1-4
18	☐ 1:5-25	☐ 1:26-46	☐ 1:47-56	☐ 1:57-80	☐ 2:1-8	☐ 2:9-20	☐ 2:21-39
19	☐ 2:40-52	☐ 3:1-20	☐ 3:21-38	☐ 4:1-13	☐ 4:14-30	☐ 4:31-44	☐ 5:1-26
20	☐ 5:27—6:16	☐ 6:17-38	☐ 6:39-49	☐ 7:1-17	☐ 7:18-23	☐ 7:24-35	☐ 7:36-50
21	☐ 8:1-15	☐ 8:16-25	☐ 8:26-39	☐ 8:40-56	☐ 9:1-17	☐ 9:18-26	☐ 9:27-36
22	☐ 9:37-50	☐ 9:51-62	☐ 10:1-11	☐ 10:12-24	☐ 10:25-37	☐ 10:38-42	☐ 11:1-13
23	☐ 11:14-26	☐ 11:27-36	☐ 11:37-54	☐ 12:1-12	☐ 12:13-21	☐ 12:22-34	☐ 12:35-48
24	☐ 12:49-59	☐ 13:1-9	☐ 13:10-17	☐ 13:18-30	☐ 13:31—14:6	☐ 14:7-14	☐ 14:15-24
25	☐ 14:25-35	☐ 15:1-10	☐ 15:11-21	☐ 15:22-32	☐ 16:1-13	☐ 16:14-22	☐ 16:23-31
26	☐ 17:1-19	☐ 17:20-37	☐ 18:1-14	☐ 18:15-30	☐ 18:31-43	☐ 19:1-10	☐ 19:11-27

Reading Schedule for the Recovery Version of the New Testament with Footnotes

Wk.	Lord's Day	Monday	Tuesday	Wednesday	Thursday	Friday	Saturday
27	☐ Luke 19:28-48	☐ 20:1-19	☐ 20:20-38	☐ 20:39—21:4	☐ 21:5-27	☐ 21:28-38	☐ 22:1-20
28	☐ 22:21-38	☐ 22:39-54	☐ 22:55-71	☐ 23:1-43	☐ 23:44-56	☐ 24:1-12	☐ 24:13-35
29	☐ 24:36-53	☐ John 1:1-13	☐ 1:14-18	☐ 1:19-34	☐ 1:35-51	☐ 2:1-11	☐ 2:12-22
30	☐ 2:23—3:13	☐ 3:14-21	☐ 3:22-36	☐ 4:1-14	☐ 4:15-26	☐ 4:27-42	☐ 4:43-54
31	☐ 5:1-16	☐ 5:17-30	☐ 5:31-47	☐ 6:1-15	☐ 6:16-31	☐ 6:32-51	☐ 6:52-71
32	☐ 7:1-9	☐ 7:10-24	☐ 7:25-36	☐ 7:37-52	☐ 7:53—8:11	☐ 8:12-27	☐ 8:28-44
33	☐ 8:45-59	☐ 9:1-13	☐ 9:14-34	☐ 9:35—10:9	☐ 10:10-30	☐ 10:31—11:4	☐ 11:5-22
34	☐ 11:23-40	☐ 11:41-57	☐ 12:1-11	☐ 12:12-24	☐ 12:25-36	☐ 12:37-50	☐ 13:1-11
35	☐ 13:12-30	☐ 13:31-38	☐ 14:1-6	☐ 14:7-20	☐ 14:21-31	☐ 15:1-11	☐ 15:12-27
36	☐ 16:1-15	☐ 16:16-33	☐ 17:1-5	☐ 17:6-13	☐ 17:14-24	☐ 17:25—18:11	☐ 18:12-27
37	☐ 18:28-40	☐ 19:1-16	☐ 19:17-30	☐ 19:31-42	☐ 20:1-13	☐ 20:14-18	☐ 20:19-22
38	☐ 20:23-31	☐ 21:1-14	☐ 21:15-22	☐ 21:23-25	☐ Acts 1:1-8	☐ 1:9-14	☐ 1:15-26
39	☐ 2:1-13	☐ 2:14-21	☐ 2:22-36	☐ 2:37-41	☐ 2:42-47	☐ 3:1-18	☐ 3:19—4:22
40	☐ 4:23-37	☐ 5:1-16	☐ 5:17-32	☐ 5:33-42	☐ 6:1—7:1	☐ 7:2-29	☐ 7:30-60
41	☐ 8:1-13	☐ 8:14-25	☐ 8:26-40	☐ 9:1-19	☐ 9:20-43	☐ 10:1-16	☐ 10:17-33
42	☐ 10:34-48	☐ 11:1-18	☐ 11:19-30	☐ 12:1-25	☐ 13:1-12	☐ 13:13-43	☐ 13:44—14:5
43	☐ 14:6-28	☐ 15:1-12	☐ 15:13-34	☐ 15:35—16:5	☐ 16:6-18	☐ 16:19-40	☐ 17:1-18
44	☐ 17:19-34	☐ 18:1-17	☐ 18:18-28	☐ 19:1-20	☐ 19:21-41	☐ 20:1-12	☐ 20:13-38
45	☐ 21:1-14	☐ 21:15-26	☐ 21:27-40	☐ 22:1-21	☐ 22:22-29	☐ 22:30—23:11	☐ 23:12-15
46	☐ 23:16-30	☐ 23:31—24:21	☐ 24:22—25:5	☐ 25:6-27	☐ 26:1-13	☐ 26:14-32	☐ 27:1-26
47	☐ 27:27—28:10	☐ 28:11-22	☐ 28:23-31	☐ Rom 1:1-2	☐ 1:3-7	☐ 1:8-17	☐ 1:18-25
48	☐ 1:26—2:10	☐ 2:11-29	☐ 3:1-20	☐ 3:21-31	☐ 4:1-12	☐ 4:13-25	☐ 5:1-11
49	☐ 5:12-17	☐ 5:18—6:5	☐ 6:6-11	☐ 6:12-23	☐ 7:1-12	☐ 7:13-25	☐ 8:1-2
50	☐ 8:3-6	☐ 8:7-13	☐ 8:14-25	☐ 8:26-39	☐ 9:1-18	☐ 9:19—10:3	☐ 10:4-15
51	☐ 10:16—11:10	☐ 11:11-22	☐ 11:23-36	☐ 12:1-3	☐ 12:4-21	☐ 13:1-14	☐ 14:1-12
52	☐ 14:13-23	☐ 15:1-13	☐ 15:14-33	☐ 16:1-5	☐ 16:6-24	☐ 16:25-27	☐ 1 Cor 1:1-4

Reading Schedule for the Recovery Version of the New Testament with Footnotes

Wk.	Lord's Day	Monday	Tuesday	Wednesday	Thursday	Friday	Saturday
53	1 Cor 1:5-9	1:10-17	1:18-31	2:1-5	2:6-10	2:11-16	3:1-9
54	3:10-13	3:14-23	4:1-9	4:10-21	5:1-13	6:1-11	6:12-20
55	7:1-16	7:17-24	7:25-40	8:1-13	9:1-15	9:16-27	10:1-4
56	10:5-13	10:14-33	11:1-6	11:7-16	11:17-26	11:27-34	12:1-11
57	12:12-22	12:23-31	13:1-13	14:1-12	14:13-25	14:26-33	14:34-40
58	15:1-19	15:20-28	15:29-34	15:35-49	15:50-58	16:1-9	16:10-24
59	2 Cor 1:1-4	1:5-14	1:15-22	1:23—2:11	2:12-17	3:1-6	3:7-11
60	3:12-18	4:1-6	4:7-12	4:13-18	5:1-8	5:9-15	5:16-21
61	6:1-13	6:14—7:4	7:5-16	8:1-15	8:16-24	9:1-15	10:1-6
62	10:7-18	11:1-15	11:16-33	12:1-10	12:11-21	13:1-10	13:11-14
63	Gal 1:1-5	1:6-14	1:15-24	2:1-13	2:14-21	3:1-4	3:5-14
64	3:15-22	3:23-29	4:1-7	4:8-20	4:21-31	5:1-12	5:13-21
65	5:22-26	6:1-10	6:11-15	6:16-18	Eph 1:1-3	1:4-6	1:7-10
66	1:11-14	1:15-18	1:19-23	2:1-5	2:6-10	2:11-14	2:15-18
67	2:19-22	3:1-7	3:8-13	3:14-18	3:19-21	4:1-4	4:5-10
68	4:11-16	4:17-24	4:25-32	5:1-10	5:11-21	5:22-26	5:27-33
69	6:1-9	6:10-14	6:15-18	6:19-24	Phil 1:1-7	1:8-18	1:19-26
70	1:27—2:4	2:5-11	2:12-16	2:17-30	3:1-6`	3:7-11	3:12-16
71	3:17-21	4:1-9	4:10-23	Col 1:1-8	1:9-13	1:14-23	1:24-29
72	2:1-7	2:8-15	2:16-23	3:1-4	3:5-15	3:16-25	4:1-18
73	1 Thes 1:1-3	1:4-10	2:1-12	2:13—3:5	3:6-13	4:1-10	4:11—5:11
74	5:12-28	2 Thes 1:1-12	2:1-17	3:1-18	1 Tim 1:1-2	1:3-4	1:5-14
75	1:15-20	2:1-7	2:8-15	3:1-13	3:14—4:5	4:6-16	5:1-25
76	6:1-10	6:11-21	2 Tim 1:1-10	1:11-18	2:1-15	2:16-26	3:1-13
77	3:14—4:8	4:9-22	Titus 1:1-4	1:5-16	2:1-15	3:1-8	3:9-15
78	Philem 1:1-11	1:12-25	Heb 1:1-2	1:3-5	1:6-14	2:1-9	2:10-18

Reading Schedule for the Recovery Version of the New Testament with Footnotes

Wk.	Lord's Day	Monday	Tuesday	Wednesday	Thursday	Friday	Saturday
79	□ Heb 3:1-6	□ 3:7-19	□ 4:1-9	□ 4:10-13	□ 4:14-16	□ 5:1-10	□ 5:11—6:3
80	□ 6:4-8	□ 6:9-20	□ 7:1-10	□ 7:11-28	□ 8:1-6	□ 8:7-13	□ 9:1-4
81	□ 9:5-14	□ 9:15-28	□ 10:1-18	□ 10:19-28	□ 10:29-39	□ 11:1-6	□ 11:7-19
82	□ 11:20-31	□ 11:32-40	□ 12:1-2	□ 12:3-13	□ 12:14-17	□ 12:18-26	□ 12:27-29
83	□ 13:1-7	□ 13:8-12	□ 13:13-15	□ 13:16-25	□ James 1:1-8	□ 1:9-18	□ 1:19-27
84	□ 2:1-13	□ 2:14-26	□ 3:1-18	□ 4:1-10	□ 4:11-17	□ 5:1-12	□ 5:13-20
85	□ 1 Pet 1:1-2	□ 1:3-4	□ 1:5	□ 1:6-9	□ 1:10-12	□ 1:13-17	□ 1:18-25
86	□ 2:1-3	□ 2:4-8	□ 2:9-17	□ 2:18-25	□ 3:1-13	□ 3:14-22	□ 4:1-6
87	□ 4:7-16	□ 4:17-19	□ 5:1-4	□ 5:5-9	□ 5:10-14	□ 2 Pet 1:1-2	□ 1:3-4
88	□ 1:5-8	□ 1:9-11	□ 1:12-18	□ 1:19-21	□ 2:1-3	□ 2:4-11	□ 2:12-22
89	□ 3:1-6	□ 3:7-9	□ 3:10-12	□ 3:13-15	□ 3:16	□ 3:17-18	□ 1 John 1:1-2
90	□ 1:3-4	□ 1:5	□ 1:6	□ 1:7	□ 1:8-10	□ 2:1-2	□ 2:3-11
91	□ 2:12-14	□ 2:15-19	□ 2:20-23	□ 2:24-27	□ 2:28-29	□ 3:1-5	□ 3:6-10
92	□ 3:11-18	□ 3:19-24	□ 4:1-6	□ 4:7-11	□ 4:12-15	□ 4:16—5:3	□ 5:4-13
93	□ 5:14-17	□ 5:18-21	□ 2 John 1:1-3	□ 1:4-9	□ 1:10-13	□ 3 John 1:1-6	□ 1:7-14
94	□ Jude 1:1-4	□ 1:5-10	□ 1:11-19	□ 1:20-25	□ Rev 1:1-3	□ 1:4-6	□ 1:7-11
95	□ 1:12-13	□ 1:14-16	□ 1:17-20	□ 2:1-6	□ 2:7	□ 2:8-9	□ 2:10-11
96	□ 2:12-14	□ 2:15-17	□ 2:18-23	□ 2:24-29	□ 3:1-3	□ 3:4-6	□ 3:7-9
97	□ 3:10-13	□ 3:14-18	□ 3:19-22	□ 4:1-5	□ 4:6-7	□ 4:8-11	□ 5:1-6
98	□ 5:7-14	□ 6:1-8	□ 6:9-17	□ 7:1-8	□ 7:9-17	□ 8:1-6	□ 8:7-12
99	□ 8:13—9:11	□ 9:12-21	□ 10:1-4	□ 10:5-11	□ 11:1-4	□ 11:5-14	□ 11:15-19
100	□ 12:1-4	□ 12:5-9	□ 12:10-18	□ 13:1-10	□ 13:11-18	□ 14:1-5	□ 14:6-12
101	□ 14:13-20	□ 15:1-3	□ 16:1-12	□ 16:13-21	□ 17:1-6	□ 17:7-18	□ 18:1-8
102	□ 18:9—19:4	□ 19:5-10	□ 19:11-16	□ 19:17-21	□ 20:1-6	□ 20:7-10	□ 20:11-15
103	□ 21:1	□ 21:2	□ 21:3-8	□ 21:9-13	□ 21:14-18	□ 21:19-21	□ 21:22-27
104	□ 22:1	□ 22:2	□ 22:3-11	□ 22:12-15	□ 22:16-17	□ 22:18-21	□

Week 7 — Day 1   Today's verses

Jer.
30:9   But they will serve Jehovah their God and David their King, whom I will raise up for them.

Hosea
3:5   Afterward the children of Israel will return and seek Jehovah their God and David their King, and they will come with fear to Jehovah and to His goodness in the last days.

_____
Date

Week 7 — Day 2   Today's verses

Matt.
12:3-4   But He said to them, Have you not read what David did when he became hungry, and those who were with him; how he entered into the house of God, and they ate the bread of the Presence, which was not lawful for him to eat, nor for those who were with him, except for the priests only?

1:6   And Jesse begot David the king.…

_____
Date

Week 7 — Day 3   Today's verses

Amos
9:11-12   In that day I will raise up the fallen tabernacle of David, and I will wall up its breaches and raise up its ruins and build it up as it was in the days of old; that they may possess the remnant of Edom and all the nations which are called by My name, declares Jehovah who does this.

_____
Date

Week 7 — Day 4   Today's verses

Matt.
13:43   Then the righteous will shine forth like the sun in the kingdom of their Father.…

25:31   But when the Son of Man comes in His glory and all the angels with Him, at that time He will sit on the throne of His glory.

_____
Date

Week 7 — Day 5   Today's verses

Isa.
22:22   And I will set the key of the house of David upon his shoulder—when he opens, no one will shut; when he shuts, no one will open.

Rev.
3:7   …These things says the Holy One, the true One, the One who has the key of David, the One who opens and no one will shut, and shuts and no one opens.

1:6   And made us a kingdom, priests to His God and Father.…

_____
Date

Week 7 — Day 6   Today's verses

Matt.
28:18   And Jesus came and spoke to them, saying, All authority has been given to Me in heaven and on earth.

Rev.
3:12   He who overcomes, him I will make a pillar in the temple of My God, and he shall by no means go out anymore, and I will write upon him the name of My God and the name of the city of My God, the New Jerusalem, which descends out of heaven from My God, and My new name.

_____
Date

Week 8 — Day 4   Today's verses

Matt. But He answered and said to them, An evil
12:39 and adulterous generation seeks after a
sign, and a sign shall not be given to it except the sign of Jonah the prophet.

41 Ninevite men will stand up in the judgment with this generation and will condemn it, because they repented at the
preaching of Jonah, and behold, something more than Jonah is here.

Date

Week 8 — Day 5   Today's verses

Eph. Abolishing in His flesh the law of the com-
2:15 mandments in ordinances, that He might
create the two in Himself into one new
man, so making peace.

17 And coming, He announced peace as the
gospel to you who were far off, and peace to
those who were near.

Date

Week 8 — Day 6   Today's verses

Jonah And I, should I not have pity on Nineveh,
4:11 the great city, in which are more than a
hundred and twenty thousand people who
cannot discern between their right hand
and their left, and many cattle?

Acts ...You shall be My witnesses both in Jeru-
1:8 salem and in all Judea and Samaria and
unto the uttermost part of the earth.

Date

Week 8 — Day 1   Today's verses

Heb. Since therefore the children have shared
2:14 in blood and flesh, He also Himself in like
manner partook of the same, that through
death He might destroy him who has the
might of death, that is, the devil.

2 Tim. ...Our Savior Christ Jesus, who nullified
1:10 death and brought life and incorruption to
light through the gospel.

Date

Week 8 — Day 2   Today's verses

Col. Stripping off the rulers and the authorities,
2:15 He made a display of them openly, triumphing over them in it.

1 Pet. For Christ also has suffered once for sins...
3:18-19 on the one hand being put to death in the
flesh, but on the other, made alive in the
Spirit; in which also He went and proclaimed to the spirits in prison.

Date

Week 8 — Day 3   Today's verses

Acts Whom God has raised up, having loosed
2:24 the pangs of death, since it was not possible for Him to be held by it.

Rev. And the living One; and I became dead,
1:18 and behold, I am living forever and ever;
and I have the keys of death and of Hades.

Date

Week 9 — Day 1   Today's verses

Matt. ...[Herod] inquired of them where the
2:4-5 Christ was to be born. And they said to
him, In Bethlehem of Judea, for so it is
written through the prophet.

Micah (But you, O Bethlehem Ephrathah, so lit-
5:2 tle to be among the thousands of Judah,
from you there will come forth to Me He
who is to be Ruler in Israel; and His
goings forth are from ancient times, from
the days of eternity.)

Date

Week 9 — Day 2   Today's verses

John In the beginning was the Word, and the
1:1 Word was with God, and the Word was
God.

51 And He said to him, Truly, truly, I say to
you, You shall see heaven opened and
the angels of God ascending and descending on the Son of Man.

Date

Week 9 — Day 3   Today's verses

John All things came into being through Him,
1:3 and apart from Him not one thing came
into being which has come into being.

14 And the Word became flesh and tabernacled among us (and we beheld His glory,
glory as of the only Begotten from the Father), full of grace and reality.

Date

Week 9 — Day 4   Today's verses

John ...Behold, the Lamb of God, who takes
1:29 away the sin of the world!

Acts This man, delivered up by the determined
2:23 counsel and foreknowledge of God, you,
through the hand of lawless men, nailed
to a cross and killed.

Date

Week 9 — Day 5   Today's verses

John ...Jesus said, You are Simon, the son of
1:42 John; you shall be called Cephas (which is
interpreted, Peter).

51 ...You shall see heaven opened and the
angels of God ascending and descending
on the Son of Man.

Date

Week 9 — Day 6   Today's verses

John And John testified, saying, I beheld the Spirit
1:32 descending as a dove out of heaven, and He
abode upon Him.

1 Cor. So also it is written, "The first man, Adam,
15:45 became a living soul"; the last Adam became a life-giving Spirit.

Date

Week 10 — Day 4   Today's verses

John 14:23   ...If anyone loves Me, he will keep My word, and My Father will love him, and We will come to him and make an abode with him.

1 Cor. 14:26   What then, brothers? Whenever you come together, each one has a psalm, has a teaching, has a revelation, has a tongue, has an interpretation. Let all things be done for building up.

_____
Date

Week 10 — Day 5   Today's verses

Hag. 2:7   And I will shake all the nations, and the Desire of all the nations will come...

Matt. 16:18   ...Upon this rock I will build My church, and the gates of Hades shall not prevail against it.

27   For the Son of Man is to come in the glory of His Father with His angels, and then He will repay each man according to his doings.

_____
Date

Week 10 — Day 6   Today's verses

Hag. 2:7   ...And I will fill this house with glory, says Jehovah of hosts.

9   The latter glory of this house will be greater than the former, says Jehovah of hosts; and in this place I will give peace, declares Jehovah of hosts.

Eph. 3:21   To Him be the glory in the church and in Christ Jesus unto all the generations forever and ever. Amen.

_____
Date

Week 10 — Day 1   Today's verses

Hag. 1:2   ...This people says, The time has not come, the time for the house of Jehovah to be built.

8   Go up to the mountain and bring wood and build the house, and I will take pleasure in it and will be glorified, says Jehovah.

_____
Date

Week 10 — Day 2   Today's verses

John 14:20   In that day you will know that I am in My Father, and you in Me, and I in you.

1 John 4:15   Whoever confesses that Jesus is the Son of God, God abides in him and he in God.

_____
Date

Week 10 — Day 3   Today's verses

Eph. 4:15-16   But holding to truth in love, we may grow up into Him in all things, who is the Head, Christ, out from whom all the Body, being joined together and being knit together through every joint of the rich supply and through the operation in the measure of each one part, causes the growth of the Body unto the building up of itself in love.

_____
Date

Week 11 — Day 4   Today's verses

Mal. 1:2 I have loved you, says Jehovah; but you say, How have You loved us? Was not Esau Jacob's brother, declares Jehovah? Yet I loved Jacob.

3:13-14 Your words have been strongly against Me, says Jehovah; but you say, What have we spoken against You? You say, It is vain to serve God; and what profit is it that we have kept His charge and have walked mournfully before Jehovah of hosts?

_____
Date

Week 11 — Day 5   Today's verses

Mal. 3:1-3 I am about to send My messenger, and he will clear the way before Me; and suddenly the Lord, whom you seek, will come to His temple. And the Angel of the covenant, whom you desire, He will come, says Jehovah of hosts. And who will endure the day of His coming? And who will stand when He appears? For He is like a refiner's fire and like fullers' soap. And He will sit as a refiner and a purifier of silver, and He will purify the sons of Levi and purge them like gold and like silver, and they will offer to Jehovah a sacrifice in righteousness.

_____
Date

Week 11 — Day 6   Today's verses

Mal. 4:2 But unto you who fear My name will the Sun of righteousness arise with healing in His wings, and you will go forth and leap about like well-fed calves.

Matt. 13:43 Then the righteous will shine forth like the sun in the kingdom of their Father....

_____
Date

Week 11 — Day 1   Today's verses

Matt. 24:3 And as He sat on the Mount of Olives, the disciples came to Him privately, saying, Tell us, When will these things be? And what will be the sign of Your coming and of the consummation of the age?

15 Therefore when you see the abomination of desolation, which was spoken of through Daniel the prophet, standing in the holy place (let him who reads understand).

_____
Date

Week 11 — Day 2   Today's verses

Matt. 24:14 And this gospel of the kingdom will be preached in the whole inhabited earth for a testimony to all the nations, and then the end will come.

Dan. 7:25 And he will speak things against the Most High and wear out the saints of the Most High...and they will be given into his hand for a time and times and half a time.

_____
Date

Week 11 — Day 3   Today's verses

Mal. 1:6-7 A son honors his father, and a servant his lord. Therefore if I am a Father, where is My honor? And if I am the Lord, where is My fear? says Jehovah of hosts to you, O priests who despise My name. But you say, How have we despised Your name? You offer defiled food upon My altar. And you say, How have we defiled You? In that you say, The table of Jehovah is despicable.

1 John 1:8 If we say that we do not have sin, we are deceiving ourselves, and the truth is not in us.

_____
Date

Week 12 — Day 4 — Today's verses

Joel
2:28-29
...I will pour out My Spirit upon all flesh, and your sons and your daughters shall prophesy; your old men shall dream dreams; your young men shall see visions....In those days I will pour out My Spirit.

Hag.
1:14
...Jehovah stirred up the spirit of Zerubbabel...and the spirit of Joshua...the high priest, and the spirit of all the remnant of the people; and they came and did work in the house of Jehovah of hosts their God.

Date _____

Week 12 — Day 5 — Today's verses

Mal.
4:2
But unto you who fear My name will the Sun of righteousness arise with healing in His wings, and you will go forth and leap about like well-fed calves.

Rev.
14:1
And I saw, and behold, the Lamb standing on Mount Zion, and with Him a hundred and forty-four thousand, having His name and the name of His Father written on their foreheads.

Date _____

Week 12 — Day 6 — Today's verses

John
21:15-17
...Jesus said..., Simon,...do you love Me...? He said to Him, Yes, Lord, You know that I love You. He said to him, Feed My lambs. He said to him again a second time, Simon,...do you love Me?...Shepherd My sheep. He said to him the third time, Simon,...do you love Me?...Feed My sheep.

Date _____

Week 12 — Day 1 — Today's verses

Hab.
3:2
...O Jehovah, revive Your work in the midst of the years; in the midst of the years make it known....

Psa.
80:17-19
Let Your hand be upon the man of Your right hand, upon the son of man whom You have strengthened for Yourself;...Revive us, and we will call upon Your name. O Jehovah God of hosts, restore us; cause Your face to shine, and we will be saved.

Date _____

Week 12 — Day 2 — Today's verses

Hosea
3:4
For the children of Israel will abide for many days without king and without prince and without sacrifice and without pillar and without ephod and teraphim.

6:1-2
Come and let us return to Jehovah; for He has torn us, but He will heal us, and He has stricken us, but He will bind us up. He will enliven us after two days; on the third day He will raise us up, and we will live in His presence.

Date _____

Week 12 — Day 3 — Today's verses

Rom.
8:22-23
For we know that the whole creation groans together and travails in pain together until now. And not only so, but we ourselves also, who have the firstfruits of the Spirit, even we ourselves groan in ourselves, eagerly awaiting sonship, the redemption of our body.

John
11:25
...I am the resurrection and the life; he who believes into Me, even if he should die, shall live.

Date _____

30   38
60 +20
90   58